THE CULT OF CANNIBALS

by
John Roy Bohlen

...you have done it to the least of these you have done it unto me."

Library of Congress Catalogue
Card Number 87-071521
ISBN # 0-9607702-1-6

Published by, for and in behalf of the
Kingdom of God.

GREAT COMMISSION MINISTRIES
P.O. Box 7123
Minneapolis, Minnesota, 55407, U.S.A.

Destiny Image Publishers
P.O. Box 351
Shippensburg, PA 17257
(717) 532-3040

CULT OF CANNIBALS

by
John Roy Bohlen

Jim Bakker?

Jerry Fallwell?

Pat Robertson?

Oral Roberts?

Kenneth Hagin?

Kenneth Copeland?

Baptists?

Catholics?

President Reagan?

Billy Graham?

Tongue Talkers?

Moral Majority?

AUTHOR'S CONTEMPLATIONS

The Bible says, "So we boiled my son and ate him; and I said to her on the next day, 'Give your son, that we may eat him'; but she has hidden her son." Here, in II Kings 6, God's people are actually doing literal physical cannibalizing!!!

The New Testament says, "But if you bite and devour one another, take care lest you be consumed by one another." Gal.2:20.

This book is about our relationships with each other. It is intended to be a handbook on rightly relating. IF YOU WILL FOLLOW THE INSTRUCTIONS IN THIS HANDBOOK ON RELATIONSHIPS, YOU WILL NEVER NEED TO WRONGLY RELATE TO ANYONE AGAIN!!!

Have you ever had any one bite you hard enough to draw blood? I have. I carry, on my leg, the teeth scars from a fight I had with my friend Gerald Underwood from the 7th grade. I remember that when my friend bit me, that it really hurt! The wounds took a long time to heal.

I wonder if the religious people actually used their teeth as murder weapons, to tear the flesh of that young evangelist there in the Bible in the book of Acts, before they stoned him?

It says, "...they gnashed on him with their teeth." Acts 7.

I wonder what Paul meant when he warned, Be careful, Dear Ones, lest "you bite and devour one another, take heed that you be not consumed of one another."

I was hunting one time in the foothills of the High Sierra Mountains when we came upon a huge rattle snake that had swallowed two and one half squirrels.

What about two snakes biting and then swallowing each other to death? I've heard Louis L'Amour talk about how many western gunfights ended in a tie. They outdrew, shot and killed each other at the same time!

I wonder what a duel would be like, with teeth as the weapon?

From what I understand, rabies is an incurable disease where whatever (or whoever) gets it, wants to bite whatever (or whoever) is around, and thus inflicts the one they bite with the disease.

I get slightly nauseated at the thought of a dog eating its young. But cannibalism????????????????? God's people actually came to this in the Bible! See Leviticus 26:29; II Kings 6:22-29; Ps.14:4; 27:2; 53:4; Jer.19:9; Lam.2:20; Ezek.5:10; Mica 3:3; Zech.11:9; and Galatians 5:15. It's true. It's really, really true. Could it happen to you? Spiritual rabies, I mean?

It happens often where Christians gather. At church, in restaurants even! The purpose of this book is to minimize cannibalism among the dear ones, and to increase our love for each other.

Oh, God! If we would only love each other!!! Oh, if we would only love each other..... Oh, Oh Please Dear God, help us to love one another. Oh dear ones, please, let's us just love each other! Please???????????

Let's not cannibalize each other any more? In Jesus' Name, Amen.

Other books or articles by the Author: (Also available on tape)

HOW TO RULE THE WORLD or *Seek 1st the Kingdom of God*
THE CULT OF CANNIBALS - Secrets for unity in God's family
THE SEXUAL MINISTRY - How marrieds can live happily ever after!
HOW TO RAISE "PURFECT" KIDS
Kingdom Contract - (An excellent handout brochure.)
"Hell Is Hot!" - An article on hell;
"The King's Greatest Secret" - included in the books above)

Other books and tapes and literature by these ministries are also available at this address just given, on the subjects of Walking in the Holy Spirit, God's Priorities, Actualizing Our Potential, Knowing the Voice of the Lord, Knowing How to See the Lord, Solutions to Family Conflicts, etc.

CULT OF CANNIBALS

TABLE OF CONTENTS

CULT OF CANNIBALS

TABLE OF CONTENTS

Then Live — The Greatest Moment Of My Life!
—Cataclysmic Revolution — The Third Coming Of
Christ?! — Inferiority Complex — The Elephant &
The Flea — The Glory Spell — A Foundation Stone!
— In His Image Questions.

Fightings Among You" — The Iowa Farm Boy —
"Messing With The Word Of God" — Faced With
The Facts!!! — Let Your Fingers Do The Talking
—The Judgment Seat Of Christ — Hello, My Brother!
Hellow, My Sister — Questions.

EPILOGUE — Humpty Dumpty Hearts Lived
Happily Ever After — God's Vision — Ours — The
Great Commission — Kingdom Questions.

ABOUT THE AUTHOR

John Roy Bohlen is nothing much, nothing at all without Christ. He likes that Scripture,"Not that we are sufficient of ourselves to think any thing as of ourselves; but our sufficiency is of God; who also has made us able ministers..." II Corinthians 3. So John thinks that if he has done something good or has accomplished something, that the credit belongs to God. He only takes the credit for the negative. That way he repents, and receives forgiveness. But here is a little account of some of his adventures with the Lord thus far in his lifetime.

Raised on "back woods" farms in southeast Iowa, (the only running water they ever had was when he or someone ran and got it), John grew up being deeply hungry to know God and walk close with Him. I suppose he had a head start in this, because his folks and ancestors, far back as they can trace, also had a deep love for God, and were born again. So, there were many times out under the stars, over on the river bank, up in the barn, or down in the woods when with his Bible, John would hunger and yearn for deeper fulfillment of the will of God in his life. He yearns still. But oh, the adventures! Mightily, he was met by God during his senior year at Bethel College in St Paul. He tells about it here. He received his B.A. in Philosophy and psychology under Dr. Bob Smith in 1961. John met Karen at Bethany Fellowship Missionary Training Center in Minneapolis from which they graduated in 1964. "Lady K." (Karen), is also a Registered X-ray Technician, and gives training to women in their ministry to their husband, children, churches and world.

God has used men like Leonard Ravenhill, Allan Langstaff, Dr. Bob Smith, along with many foundational ministries, and prophets, intercessors and enemies as an encouragement. John was a probation officer for L. A. County for 6 years, and has known various phases of construction and real estate. The Bohlen's have helped establish a number of churches in Arizona, Nebraska, California, Minnesota, etc., and pioneered and pastored metropolitan churches in Phoenix and Minneapolis. Two 40-day fasts and much seeking of God has resulted in the establishing of ministries focusing on the Great Commission, Knowing the Will of God, and Actualizing Our Potential in God.

John and Karen are blessed with four children: Joseph, Kari, Dawn Joy and Joshua. The family travels extensively and they minister the Word, sing as a family, conduct Seminars with others of a similar vision on: The Great Commission, Finding and Fulfilling Our Destiny in God, Marriage and the Family, Equipping the Saints, and Worship. These seminars are available in your area, world wide.

John has also written a book, *"How To Rule The World" or "Seek 1st The Kingdom of God"* which has had tremendous receptivity around the world! It is an excellent handbook on discipleship and is also ideal for a teaching series. Other books are available on marriage, The Sexual Ministry, and the family, *How To Raise "Purfect" Kids!* (These may be ordered from K.O.G., P.O. Box 7123, Mpls., MN., 55407.) A 6 hour Seminar on God's Priorities, divided into 30 minute segments, will soon be available on video tape, God providing. The book, *How To Rule The World or Seek 1st The Kingdom Of God* is also available on tape, as well as other tapes, such as "The King's Greatest Secret!", "Helping Heal Hurting Humpty-Dumpty Hearts," "I Corinthians 14:26", etc.

DEDICATION

Jesus Christ, Mighty God, Yahweh, I dedicate this book to You. Please forgive me for every time that I mistreated the least of these Your brothers, 'cause when I did it to them I did it to You!

This book is lovingly dedicated to all "Christian" cannibals and vampires everywhere... to Helen, Ken, Don, Dianne, Jimmy, Dave, David, T.H., Lowell, Fred, Fred, and Sheila, Len, etc. We pray that soon, very soon you'll come out from among..."THE CULT OF CANNIBALS"!!! Also, please take note, that "WHEN YOU DID IT TO THE LEAST OF THE DISCIPLES, THEN YOU DID IT TO JESUS"! (Matt.25).

We dedicate this book as well to the dear ones who have been hurt by the cannibals. To those of you who are still bleeding, hurt, or broken, may the Son of Righteousness arise with healing in His Wings. To those of you who have been healed of the hurt, the crown awaits you, IF you stay right in your spirit. WHEN THEY DID IT TO YOU, THEY DID IT TO CHRIST!

To those that have died, or whose ministries or reputations or nerves or spirits or minds or hearts have been hurt beyond recovery, take courage, for it will all be straightened out at the judgement seat of Christ!!! " 'Vengeance is Mine. I will repay!' saith the Lord!" Rom.12:9. (Except for those who still have time to repent and will take the time to do so.) IT HAS BEEN ACCREDITED TO THEIR ACCOUNT AS HAVING BEEN DONE TO THE CHRIST!!!

To those of you who have never been cannibalized, when they try, (and be sure, they will, if you are walking close to the Lord), may you always keep a right spirit, for WHEN THEY ATTACK YOU, THEY ARE ATTACKING THE CHRIST!

The majority of the artwork was done by the Lord, through the loving life of Becky Meyers. Thanks Becky!

Artwork taken from *How To Rule The World* was done by Chris Wold Dyrud.

Finally, to those of you who have steadfastly refused to cannibalize your brothers (and sisters) in Christo, but instead have only been a blessing, remember, IT HAS BEEN ACCREDITED TO YOUR ACCOUNT AS HAVING BEEN DONE TO CHRIST!!!

QUESTIONNAIRE

This questionnaire has a two-fold purpose: 1. As a teaching aid to help one ask questions so that when the answer comes, it will remain more firmly fixed. 2. To provide a "before and after" perspective so that progress may be more fully appreciated.

1. LIST YOUR REQUIREMENTS FOR FELLOWSHIPPING WITH PEOPLE.
2. LIST YOUR REQUIREMENTS FOR FELLOWSHIPPING WITH CHRISTIANS.
3. DEFINE THE FOLLOWING TERMS:
   a. Cult,
   b. Occult,
   c. Christian?
4. HOW DOES ONE BECOME A CHRISTIAN?
5. (a) IF YOU WERE PASTOR OF A CHURCH OR LEADER OF A HOME BIBLE STUDY GROUP, WHAT STANDARD OF REQUIREMENTS WOULD YOU REQUIRE SOMEONE TO MEET BEFORE THEY WOULD BE ALLOWED TO SPEAK OR BRING A MESSAGE IN YOUR MEETING?

(b) IF JESUS OR THE APOSTLE PAUL AS STRANGERS & DRESSED UP IN MODERN SUITS, CAME INTO YOUR GROUP OR CHURCH, WOULD THEY BE ALLOWED TO MINISTER?

6. IF WE SEE A PERSON IN ERROR, WHAT ARE WE TO DO, IF ANYTHING?

7. UNDER WHAT CIRCUMSTANCES IS BACKBITING ALLOWED?

8. UNDER WHAT CIRCUMSTANCES IS GOSSIP ALLOWED?

9. IS CRITICISM EVER JUSTIFIED? WHEN?

10. WHAT GROUPS OR DIVISIONS DOES GOD SEE AMONG CHRISTIANS WHEN HE LOOKS UPON THEM TODAY?

11. WOULD IT EVER BE RIGHT TO REFUSE TO EAT WITH SOMEONE? IF SO WHEN?

12. WOULD IT EVER BE RIGHT TO REFUSE TO ALLOW A CHRISTIAN TO BE IN OUR HOME, OR TO FELLOWSHIP WITH THEM OR TO NOT ALLOW THEM INTO OUR CHURCH? IF SO, WHEN?

13. WHAT DOES IT MEAN TO "BLASPHEME THE HOLY SPIRIT"?

14. WHAT IS A "HERETIC"?

15. SERIOUSLY, DO YOU KNOW ALL THERE IS TO KNOW ABOUT GOD YET?

16. WHAT DOES IT MEAN "JUDGE NOT, LEST YOU BE JUDGED"?

17. HOW DOES ONE "TRY THE SPIRITS"?

18. WHAT DO WE DO ABOUT A PERSON WHO IS DECEIVED?
19. WHAT WOULD YOUR REACTION BE IF SOME ONE ACCUSED YOU OF BEING DECEIVED? ARE YOU?
20. WHAT DOES IT MEAN TO BE DECEIVED?
21. IS THERE A DIFFERENCE BETWEEN "WRONG DOCTRINE" AND "FALSE DOCTRINE"? IF SO, WHAT?
22. HOW CAN A PERSON TELL IF ANOTHER PERSON OR GROUP OR TEACHING OR BOOK IS NOT OF GOD?
23. WHAT DOES JESUS MEAN: "IN AS MUCH AS YOU HAVE DONE IT UNTO THE LEAST OF THESE MY BRETHREN, YOU HAVE DONE IT UNTO ME."?
24. WHO ARE THE "BRETHREN", IN THIS CASE?
25. UNDER WHAT CONDITIONS SHOULD YOU "BREAK FELLOWSHIP" WITH A FELLOW MEMBER OF THE BODY OF CHRIST?
26. WHAT WOULD YOU SAY IS THE PROPER PROCEDURE IF YOU HAVE A GRIEVANCE OR PROBLEM WITH YOUR FELLOW MEMBER (S) IN THE BODY OF CHRIST?
27. IF YOUR BROTHER "OFFENDS" YOU, WHAT SHOULD YOU DO?
28. IF YOUR BROTHER HAS SOMETHING AGAINST YOU, WHAT SHOULD YOU DO?

29. IF YOU HEAR, BACKBITING, GOSSIP, TALE BEARING, OR SLANDER, ETC, WHAT SHOULD YOU DO, IF ANYTHING?

30. IF YOU BELIEVE THAT A CERTAIN MINISTER IS WRONG, WHAT SHOULD YOU DO?

31. IF YOU WERE PASTOR OF A CHURCH, OR WERE RESPONSIBLE FOR A HOME GROUP, WOULD YOU ALLOW SOMEONE TO COME TO IT, OR MINISTER, IF THEY DISAGREED WITH YOU ABOUT THE FOLLOWING THINGS?:

(1) THE RAPTURE
(2) WATER BAPTISM
(3) ETERNAL SECURITY
(4) PROSPERITY?
(5) SURVIVAL OR FOOD STORAGE?
(6) CONFIRMATION?
(7) THE TRINITY - VS "JESUS ONLY"
(8) CHURCH GOVERNMENT?
(9) DIVORCE?
(10) ORAL SEX?
(11) MOVIES?
(12) AURAS?
(13) JERRY FALLWELL?
(14) TONGUES?
(15) HAVING JEWELRY, CARS OR RADIOS?
(16) SNAKE HANDLING AS PART OF THEIR WORSHIP?
(17) INSPIRATION OF THE SCRIPTURES?
(18) WAS JESUS ACTUALLY GOD?

(19) CAN WE BE LIKE GOD OR PERFECT THIS SIDE OF DEATH?

(20) IS THE BIBLE THE WORD OF GOD?

(21) IF YOUR FRIENDS WERE SUSPICIOUS OF THIS PERSON?

(22) IF YOU HAD HEARD BAD THINGS ABOUT THIS PERSON?

(23) IF YOU HAD NEVER SEEN OR HEARD OF THIS PERSON BEFORE?

(24) IF THEY DID NOT BELIEVE IN "ETERNAL SECURITY"?

(25) IF THEY BELIEVED THAT A CHRISTIAN COULD BE DEMON POSSESSED?

32. TRUTHFULLY, DO YOU THINK YOU ARE BETTER THAN OTHERS?

EXPLANATION

—Unless otherwise noted: all Scriptures are quoted from the New American Standard Bible. The Lockman Foundation — 1960, 1962, 1963, 1971, 1972, 1973, 1975, are used by permission.
—All quotations from the King James Version are identified as (KJ).
—All author's paraphrases or adaptions are identified as (JB).
—All quotations from the Amplified New Testament are identified as (AMP), and are also used by permission from the Lockman Foundation, © 1958.

INTRODUCTION

Have you ever been mistreated? Have you ever been intimidated? Have you ever been falsely accused? Have people ever gossiped about you? Do you still carry the scars, hurts, wounds or bleedings from these mistreatments? Would you like to know how to handle any future situations like these? Would you like to know how to be healed from these hurts?

This book has the answer for life's greatest problems— including HOW TO RIGHTLY RELATE TO EACH OTHER!!!

Saint Peter said, "ABOVE ALL, love each other fervently from a pure heart!" I P.1:22 & 4:8 (JB).

Apostle Paul said, "ALL of the law IS FULFILLED in this: that you love your neighbor as yourself." Gal.5:14 (JB).

KING YESHUA said, "By THIS shall all men know that you are My disciples, IF YOU LOVE EACH OTHER." John 13:35.

Yet, someone has said that the only army that buries its wounded are Christians!

This book deals with questions like:

What is the basis on my acceptance or rejection of someone?

What is the basis of my acceptance of rejection of someone?
If I feel critical of someone, what should I do?
If I have been mistreated, what recourse do I have?

(SEE ALSO THE QUESTIONNAIRE HERE AT THE BEGINNING, AND NOTE THE QUESTIONS FOLLOWING EACH CHAPTER.)

We are recommending that every school not only teach people how to learn, remember, and memorize, but that every school have a course on ....
RELATING!!!!!!
The questionnaire given here, as well as the of chapters, number and the questions following every chapter, are also intended for study situations, for the church, the school, or for personal study. May you have fun as you learn.

CHAPTER 1 — OUTLINE

PURPOSE

I. PURPOSE OF THIS BOOK

II. SELECTED SCRIPTURES ON CANNIBALISM

III. REVIEW

1

THE PURPOSE OF
THIS BOOK

We become outraged at murder, yet we Christians are guilty of the most grisly of murder, mayhem, maiming, mugging, and many multitudinous monstrosities!!!

Let me explain: There is a hideous problem among Christians today that must be solved, or, according to the last verses of the Old Testament, God is going to come and "Smite the earth with a curse"! That problem is disunity, criticism, back biting, and the sowing of discord among the brethren. The implications of this criticism are terrifyingly far reaching. Someone has said that far more people have been murdered by the tongue than by all the other instruments of war combined! (See James 3).

We are called and dedicated to see healing of hearts and relationships take place in the body of Christ. Remember, Jesus said, "Inasmuch as you have done it even unto one of the least of these My brethren, you have done it unto Me." Matthew 25. They actually did it to Jesus!!!

Therefore this book is intended as a handbook on HOW TO RIGHTLY RELATE TO EACH OTHER in the body of Christ! The Army of God is described in Joel chapter 2. "They shall not break their ranks:" "Neither shall one thrust another; they shall march every one in his path..."(Verses 7b & 8a). I so wish that this could be said for us modern Christians. Jesus said, "By this shall all know that you are My disciples, If you have love for one another"! (John 13:35) Wow! What a key for world evangelism! God commands, "Above all, love each other fervently, from pure hearts"! (1 Peter 1:22 & 4:8 - JB), and "Guard earnestly the unity of the Spirit in the bond of peace"! (Eph.4:3). In other words, it is not enough for us to simply accept, or tolerate or like or even love each other, but that we must love each other with a radiant fervent burning love that is pure.

SELECTED SCRIPTURES ON CANNIBALISM

Consider the following Scriptures:

1. Take heed, my brethren, lest ye bite and devour one another, and are consumed of one another." (Gal.5:15) How cannibalistic!

2. If you cause one of these little ones to stumble, it would be better if you had never been born." (Jesus is talking to Christians! Mk.9:42)

3. Jesus said, "If you hurt one of these little ones, it would be better for you if you had a millstone hung around your neck, and that you be dumped into the deepest part of the sea." (Matt.18:6) I wonder why this is - - -.

30

4. If you call your brother (or sister) a fool, a liar, or an idiot, you are in danger of hell fire. (Words of Jesus in Matthew 5) Whew!

5. In as much as ye have done it unto one of the least of these My brethren, you did it to Me." (Jesus) Notice, it's NOT "like" doing it unto Christ, but DOING it unto Christ!!! (Matt.25:40)

6. These ... things doth the Lord hate, yea, ... are an abomination unto Him...he that sows discord among the brethren." (Proverbs 6:16-20).

7 For if you will not forgive your brother his trespass against you, neither will your Heavenly Father forgive you." (1st promise after the Lord's prayer. Matt.6:15)

8. I John 3:15 "Whosoever hates his brother is a murderer; and you know that no murderer has eternal life abiding in him." Do you hate any of your brothers or sisters in Christ?

9. I John 3:14b "He who does not love his brother abides in death."

10. Railers...shall not inherit the Kingdom of God." (1 Cor. 6:10) Have you heard any "railing" (heavy criticism) lately? I was outraged one time upon hearing of the torture and dismembering and murder of a little girl. In the midst of my righteous anger, the Lord gently reminded me that far more serious crimes are daily done by outwardly sweet sisters and nice ladies and gentleman who verbally or spiritually or psychically murder and dismember others in the body of Christ! Have you heard the

expression for Sunday dinner?" (Sweet smiles in church—critical of the preacher over the noon meal.)

11. Mark them who cause division in the body of Christ and have nothing to do with them." (Rom.16:17)

So, this book is a declaration of war against cannibalism in the body of Christ. Which side of this war are you on?

The second reason for this book is to present a clear vision of the Church of Jesus Christ as God intended for Her to be, and to clearly show how we can be a vibrant fruitful part of THE PERFECT BRIDE!!!

CHAPTER ONE — REVIEW

1. What do you think is the purpose of this book?

2. What are the two things mentioned here about Joel's Army, (Joel 2) that speak of unity in the body of Christ?

3. Who and what did Christ mean when He said, "When you did it to _____ you did it to Me!"?

4. What is the major proof of our discipleship?

5. What key for world evangelization is given here?

6. Why is it not enough for us to just "tolerate" or like or even love one another?

7. What do we mean, "Christian" cannibalism?

8. Who are the "little ones" we must not stumble?

9. What does it mean, "cause them to stumble"?

10. What does it say we deserve if we do stumble them?

11. What are we in danger of if we call our brother or sister what?

12. Who are "these My brethren" Jesus spoke of in the sheep & goats parable?

13. What was the one of the seven things God hates as an abomination?

14. Can you find a hidden potential curse in or near the Lord's prayer?

15. Whoever hates brother or sister is a _____?

16. What in the church is as bad as, or perhaps even worse than, the dismembering of a little girl?

17. Can you think of a time when you are to have nothing to do with a fellow believer?

18. Are you willing to try to do something to stop cannibalism in the Body of Christ?

19. How have you personally been injured by the criticism of others?

Chapter 2 - Outline

"CHRISTIAN WITCHCRAFT"

I. Christian Witchcraft

II. "Little Orphan Audrey"

III. Psychic Intimidation

IV. Power Of The Tongue

V. Review

2

"CHRISTIAN" WITCHCRAFT

Before you read further, I want to explain that the following few sentences do not make very pleasant reading, but I believe it is necessary to keep you from an even greater guilt, so please bear with me. We have a dear friend, whom we shall call "Little Orphan Audrey", who was raped and mutilated by her father, and was also brutally tortured by a mother in some of the following ways: 1. Often tied in a barn all night. 2. Tied to a bed and repeatedly branded with a red hot iron. 3. Sold to be photographed while being gang raped. 4. Tied to a chair and left for hours in a closet with rats, mice and snakes. 5. Beaten over the head and body with stove wood, clubs, hammers and boards with nails. 6. Her feet were broken with hammers and her nails pulled with pliers.

In the midst of these horrible things, she invited Jesus Christ into her life to be her Saviour, Lord, and Life, and has since become a radiant happy Christian woman. She has a fabulous ministry to the retarded, the shut in's, the illiterate, the delinquent, the poor, the abused, the aged, the children, the lonely, and the Body of Christ at large. But she has an interesting confession. She states that all of the pain she experienced (at the hands of her parents, and of unsaved people in general) is NOTHING by comparison to the hideous torture and heart pain and rejection and misunderstanding and gossip and criticism she has experienced at the hands of her brothers and sisters in Christ!

For example, at the time this girl's mother sold her to be gang raped, others stood by taking pictures which are still being circulated twenty years later. These pictures are sent anonymously to churches and friends that know her. One church was especially dear to her, where she had found friends and where she was ministering. Many children were being born again and inviting Christ into their lives as a result of Audrey's ministry. Then, one day she was called before the board of elders where the pastor showed one of these revealing pictures that had been sent to him. She was accused, judged and condemned without opportunity to explain, and she was removed form her place of ministering to the children. This kind of thing has happened repeatedly.

Here's another example before we go on. A "prophet" friend of mine was coming to Minneapolis to minister. He has been used by the Lord to raise the dead and many other wonderful miracles. But during one of his first meetings, he happened to refer to Elisha's comment in II Kings 5:26, "Did not my spirit go with thee when...", or to St. Paul's comments like,

"While being absent from you in body, yet present in spirit..." I Cor. 5:3. Someone misunderstood and began spreading the story that the brother was preaching a cultic doctrine of "astral projection", or "soul travel" and that he was a false prophet and was of the devil. Other "Christian" cannibals began spreading this and other stories about this man, and many people and doors that would have otherwise been open to his valuable ministry were closed. The responsibility of all those who WOULD HAVE BEEN born again or healed or other wise met by the Lord, or whose marriages would have been saved as a result of the Lord's ministry through this brother will be upon the heads of these cannibals on the day of judgement unless there is repentance and, perhaps, forgiveness.

But these examples are only two out of many billions of bloody gossipings and back bitings done by sweet cannibalistic "Christians" in the name of our gentle and Loving Saviour who hates those "that sow discord among the brethren".

Look at this Scripture, Proverbs 6:16 to 19 and let it strike godly fear to your hearts, those of you who are vicious and bloody cannibals:

"There are six things which the Lord hates; yea seven which are an abomination unto Him: Haughty eyes, (pride), a lying tongue, (misrepresents the facts, stretches the truth) and hands that shed innocent blood, (yeah) a heart that devises wicked imaginations, (uh huh), feet that are swift in running to mischief, (some let their fingers do the running), a false witness who speaks lies, and HE WHO SOWS

38

DISCORD AMONG BROTHERS." (parenthetical comments mine).

Did you know, were you aware that God ACTUALLY HATES some people?

"CHRISTIAN WITCHCRAFT"

Would you please read that again? Only this time, apply it spiritually and psychologically, (if the shoe fits).

Where does "Christian" witchcraft come in? Do you remember the Scripture, "What ever you bind will be bound, and what ever you loose will be loosed?" Please remember that there is power in the tongue!!! The Apostle Paul wouldn't have given us that advice to not bite or devour or consume each other if it would not have been possible for us to do so!!! Galatians 5:15. Also in this chapter God says that if we are guilty of enmity, (hostility), strife, jealousy, anger, stubbornness, sedition, (incitement to discontent or rebellion) or envyings - that we will not inherit the Kingdom of God!!!

And in Ephesians 6 where it talks about being clothed with all the armor of God, please notice that not one provision is made for protection for our back or from back biting or back stabbing. We have no protective armor for our back! Are we truly at each other's mercy?

CRABBY CHRISTIANS

Someone has said that one does not need to put a lid on a bucket of crabs, for as soon as one makes some progress up the side, the other crabs reach up and pull it down. Do you know any "Christian crabs" like this - in your church, your home, or your shoes?!.

Why does the Bible say that we are guilty of murder if we hate our brother or sister? Because, in a witchcraft sense, there is a murderously destructive force unleashed against our fellow Christians when there is hatred in our hearts!

Why does the Lord tell us that we are to not give our gift to the Lord until we have first made everything right with our brother that has something against us? The answer is that there are laws in the spirit realm just like there are laws in the natural realm that can be followed or broken by saint and sinner alike. The law of gravity, for example, can be used or abused by the good guys or the bad guys; but so can every other spiritual law. In fact, the demons and witches are simply, in many ways hitchhiking on principles that God has established. If a witch or a "Christian" either one, hates someone, he or she simply focuses that hate on one so hated, often with destructive result. The destruction is increased in proportion to the intensity, the voicing of it and the action connected with it. The problem increases when "Christian" prayers and Scriptures are used, as is often the case. In fact, many devil worshippers and witches do the same! The reason that the problem is much much more serious among Christians, is that we are "members of each other"! We are one with each other! It is because of our unity that spiritual rabies is so terrifying, so damaging — like aids, like herpes simplex 2!

40

We would like to encourage you to read the New Testament again, but this time to look for the principles in the Spirit realm that affect our attitudes and relationships with each other.

We know personally of a number of families that have been broken apart because of the misguided prayers and prophesies of friends, giving crude crass cruddy counsel contrary crosswise considering Christ's commands! These families are still split as of this writing.

I actually know of "Christians" who have been praying for years for someone to die because they did not like the way that someone acted. Do you think this is bad? Remember that praying destructively for any person, group or situation outside of the will of God is a form of "Christian" witchcraft! We are defining witchcraft as "the use of any supernatural or psychic power for a purpose that is not of God." Some so-called—"Christians" do this carelessly, and often. Do you?

PSYCHIC INTIMIDATION

One of the most common forms of "Christian" witchcraft used, besides criticism, is the use of what we call "psychic intimidation". By "psychic" we simply mean "that which is of the soul, (including our emotions, feelings, suspicions, human "witnesses", hunches, thoughts and prejudices); as opposed to that which is of the Spirit of God". And by "intimidation", we mean "the attempt to influence or motivate others through any wrong form of threat or fear, including the wrong withholding of friendship or fellowship,

41

acceptance or approval". All forms of human intimidation are wrong! Love and intimidation cannot co-exist. It is amazing how many husbands woo and win their wives through sweetness, woo-ing and romance, but WITHOUT any intimidation, yet as soon as they are married, think they have a license to bully and intimidate, then wonder where her love and respect have gone. (See our book on marriage, "The Sexual Ministry.")

As an example of psychic intimidation, let's say someone says or does something of which we disapprove or about which we disagree, but that it does not come under the category of sin or is not contrary to the Bible. Many times, we will be guilty of psychic intimidation through our withheld fellowship or friendship or through some form of disfavor. This is not fair, just or right. Every man and woman must have the right, (and DOES have the responsibility), to determine the will of God for themselves. Unless it is expressly forbidden in the Bible, or unless it is physically, mentally, morally or spiritually harmful, we are to allow each other to have the freedom to find and to fulfill the will of God for themselves. In one sense, it is not enough for us to only accept Jesus as our Lord. It is also necessary that we accept Jesus as the Lord of our brother and sister. God says, "Who art thou that judgest another man's servant?" (here, it means "He's God's servant, so who do you think you are to mess with him?"), "To his own Master (here it means the Lord Jesus) he standeth or falleth. Yea, he shall be held up: for God is able to make him stand." Romans 14:4. And here's a funny one, (unless you're guilty), from Proverbs 26, "He that meddleth in a matter not his own is as one who takes a mad dog by the ears"! (JB).

POWER OF THE TONGUE

We used to raise chickens on the farm. I can still visualize (oops, did I use a naughty word?) something they would do, when one chicken would be wounded, or develop a sore, the rest of the chickens would peck it to death. Typical of chickens, but in the Family of God????? Someone has said that we Christians are the only army in the world that buries its wounded!

Are you familiar with the term "character assassination"? Someone has said that more people have been killed by the power of the tongue than by all of earth's wars put together!!! Let me ask you, how many people have you given the "Judas Kiss" to in the last week? Some parents criticize the pastor or the church in front of the children, and then wonder why the kids have no respect for God or His people now, or later.

In James 3, God says, "Out of the same mouth proceedeth blessing and cursing. My brethren, these things ought not so to be." "Doth a fountain send forth at the same place sweet water and bitter?" "But if ye have bitter envying and strife in your hearts, glory not, and lie not against the truth." "This wisdom descendeth not from above, but is earthly, sensual, devil-ISH." "For where envying and strife is, there is confusion and every evil work." "But the wisdom that is from above is first pure, then peaceable, gentle, and easy to be entreated, full of mercy and good fruits,

43

without partiality, and without hypocrisy." "And the fruit of righteousness is sown in peace of them that make peace." James 3:10,11,14-18.

Now, this next chapter is the most important chapter in this book! Please please please reach into God to learn "The Secret" where you live!!!!!!! Please leave no stone unturned until you know deep down in your guts ———- THE KING'S GREATEST SECRET!!!

CHAPTER 2 — REVIEW

1. Do you think you understand Audrey's statement about experiencing far more pain at the hands of "Christians" than at the hands of the unsaved? (She, of course is born again, that is, has asked Christ into her heart and life and has turned her whole life over to Him as Lord. Will you pause for a very important moment, and do the same?!)

2. How do you think your relatives, friends, church or work associates would react if pictures of you being sodomized or raped were sent to them?

3. Do you think YOU would have condemned Audrey, not having known the story?

4. Would you like to read her story? (We're thinking of writing a book.)

5. Of the list of 6 or 7 things that God hates, how many of them come under the general topic of "Christian" cannibalism?

6. Of the things listed here from Galatians 5:19-21, (that will get people kicked, or kept out of, the Kingdom of God), how many of them fall under the general category of "Christian" cannibalism?

7. DO you feel "vulnerable", or at least slightly dismayed that you are open to being hurt by your brothers or sisters?

8. Why is hatred equal to murder in the eyes of God? (I Jn.3:15)

9. Define "Christian" witchcraft.

10. What is meant by psychic intimidation?

11. Try to give an example of psychic intimidation from your own experience.

12. Why is it not enough (in a sense) for us only to receive Jesus as OUR Lord?

13. What is meant by "character assassination"?

14. What is meant by the "Judas Kiss"?

15. (Opinion question). Do you think it is possible to be perfect?

16. Please list, if you can, 4 to 7 of the most important things Christ took of ours with Him to the cross.

Chapter 3 — Outline

THE KING'S GREATEST SECRET

I. The King's Greatest Secret

II. How To Be Perfect!

III. The Greatest Moment Of My Life!

IV. Cataclysmic Revolution

V. Review

3

THE KING'S GREATEST SECRET
or
HOW TO BE PERFECT

God has a Secret!!! He would like to tell it to You!
The angels and men of God wanted to know this
Secret, but God wouldn't tell them for thousands of
years. Then God told The Secret to the Church
through the Apostle Paul and the other apostles and
prophets. That Secret was lost and forgotten again
during the dark ages, but now is being told again in
this special time to the Church. It's the King's
Greatest Secret! It needs to be told so very much.
Almost no one in the Church today knows The Secret.
We have ministered in many churches across the
country and in most of them we ask a certain question
to find out if they know The Secret. And in none of
the places where we have ministered had they known.
The question we asked them was, "What did Jesus
take of ours with Him to the cross?" Will you take a
minute to answer this before you continue?

We get answers, all of them correct but not
complete, like "He took our sins, our sicknesses, our

worries, burdens, fears etc." We say, "That's true that He took these so we can be forgiven, healthy, and without worry (some folks cast their burdens upon Yahweh, the Mighty Right NOW God, but as a fisherman casts, they sit and reel these burdens back to themselves.) But the people still have not told the main thing Christ took with Him to the cross! I suppose the reason they do not know, is that it requires a revelation of God, or one who has a revelation from God, to share The Secret, before they can know. What a Wonderful Mystery!

MOUNT PO-PO-KAT-A-MA-TEL or, "THE LONG DISTANCE GOD"

We believe that more than 9,999 Christians out of 10,000 relate to God in one of the following incorrect ways:

They relate to God "long distance". That is, they visualize God as living way out beyond Mount Popokatapetel somewhere, and that if they pray real long and loud and hard, that maybe God will hear them, and that maybe, but less likely, the answer will get back. The song says that Jesus leans out over the battlements of heaven, and yells down the distance, " 'Hold the fort, for I am coming', Jesus signals still. Wave the answer back to heaven, 'By Thy grace we will.' "

The other incorrect (We shall see in a moment why these are incorrect), concept of God is that of "A little bitty God inside of a BIG person with still BIGGER problems". We invite Jesus to come into our hearts, and so He does, not as our very LIFE, in most cases,

49

but as a sometimes-thought-of "Guest". (I don't like, nor will I say that prayer, "Come, Lord Jesus, be our guessed...") I don't want Him to be a guest, I want Him to come in as the Master, my very LIFE!!! But some of us, when we pray to Jesus hiding way down deep in our hearts somewhere, we get our own echoes back as if we were talking into a well. But God wants to be very Very VERY much more real to us than this.

THE SECRET!!!

The Secret is found in plain sight in a multitude of places in the Bible, especially in places like John 17, Ephesians, Romans, Galatians, Colossians, etc. BEWARE that when you hear this Secret, that you not think too lightly or casually. The proof that you got the Secret will be that you will be able to consistently keep your heart and attitude and spirit right. In fact, if you REALLY get the Secret, as the following Scriptures indicate, there will be no difference between who Christ is at the Father's right hand, and who He is - - - in you!

The Secret Mystery is this: When Christ went to the cross, He took US with Him there! When He died, WE died! When He was buried, WE were buried with ALL of our insufficiencies, inadequacies, inferiorities, insecurities, inabilities, and instabilities!!!! Everything negative, nasty, weak, or sinful about us, He took to the cross because He took US to the cross. Oh, dear one, if you grasp hold of this Secret it will make all the difference in the world for you! It will mean the difference between Christ living your life, and you living your life; between you trying to speak good things, and Christ speaking His words through you!

Lord Jesus, please make this plain and understandable. We believe together that You will make the Mystery clear. "I praise Thee, O Father, Lord of heaven and earth, that Thou didst hide these things from the wise and intelligent, and didst reveal them to babes. Yes, Father for thus it was well pleasing in Thy sight" Matt. 11:25 and Luke 10:21.

Please let me tell you more about The Secret. When The Lord Jesus Christ went to the cross, He took you with Him there! YOU WERE THERE when they crucified my Lord! Christ looked ahead in time and saw you and decided that He could not help you any other way, that He could not beat or bless you into being what He wants you to be, could not educate or "religious" you adequately, but that the only hope for you was to take you with Him to the Cross and kill you dead, along with all of your negative nature and qualities, and bury you. Unlike many self-help books, Christ does not try to get you to "hype" or hypnotize, "con" or convince yourself into thinking that you are really good or nice, adequate or o.k., but that you are horribly hopeless and hideously helpless, apart from Christ taking you to the cross with Him and putting all of your self to death and burying it in the tomb with Him. So you do not need to kill yourself or commit suicide, nor do your friends, because Jesus Christ lovingly killed us softly already. But that is not the end of the story!

**WOW! YOU REALLY ARE
SOMETHING AFTER ALL!!!**

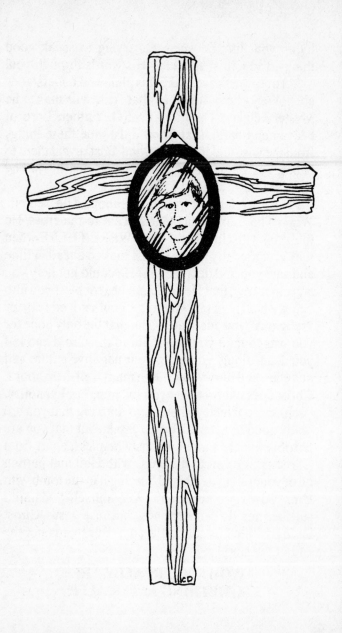

When Christ rose from the tomb HE RAISED US UP as a whole, new, beautiful, wonderful, adequate, sufficient, glorious, superior, perfect, able, stable, secure creation in His image in newness of Life so He could come into us and BE our Life, Live our Life, BE our perfection, BE our righteousness!!!

Perhaps you would like to see this Secret in the Scriptures. The following Verses can become attainable in the practical realm of the nitty gritty now:

I Cor. 15:57	Victory
II Cor. 2:14-16	Victory always everywhere
Rom. 6:7,18,22	Free from sin
Col. 3:1-3	Risen with Christ our life
Eph. 2:6	Seated in Christ
Ps. 16:11	Fullness of joy; joy unspeakable
Ps.91	Secret Place of the Most High
Eph. 1:3,4	Every blessing
Ne. 8:10	Joy of the Lord - strength
I Cor. 2:16	Mind of Christ
Ph. 4:13	Can do all things through Christ
Jude 24	Walk blamelessly
Matt. 28:18	All power and authority
Matt. 5:14	We are the light of the World
Ph. 1:21	To Live Is Christ

II Cor. 9:8	All power and authority
John 14:13	What ever we ask
John 10:10	Abundant Life
II Pet. 1:1-4	We have all things for life
Rom. 8:37	More than conquerors
I John 4:17	We are as He is
Matt. 19:26	All things are possible
I John 2:6	We can know the mysteries of the Kingdom of God
Col. 1:25-29	Mystery of the gospel of the ages
I Cor. 1:30	Christ is made unto us wisdom, righteousness, sanctification and redemption.

Galatians 2:20 says, "I have been crucified with Christ, and it is no longer I who live, BUT CHRIST LIVES IN ME!!!" In Colossians, God says that CHRIST IS OUR LIFE! The Bible says, "For me to live IS Christ" (Phil. 1:21), and "We HAVE the mind of Christ" (I Cor. 2:16), and "As He [Christ] is SO ARE WE IN THIS WORLD" I John 4:17. Oh, dear heart, I pray for you with deep, unutterable longing and faith "That the God of our Lord Jesus Christ, the Father of Glory, may give you a spirit of wisdom and of revelation in the knowledge of Him! I pray that the eyes of your heart may be enlightened so that you may KNOW..." (Eph. 1:17,18.)

THE ROAD TO HELL IS
PAVED WITH GOOD EXCUSES

Do you realize that if God Himself stepped down from a fluffy white cloud and offered an easy way for us to be perfect, that many Christians would simply not be interested?! The "Good News" message, (that we can walk before the Lord pleasing in motive, thought, word and deed), would be, to many "Christians", very "bad news". A major reason is that they want an excuse for their sinning! Another reason is that they would have to change their "doctrine" and when it comes to doctrine, some folks would rather go to hell than switch!

I have gone from door to door trying to persuade people to invite Jesus Christ into their hearts as their Lord, as a necessary FIRST step in escaping the eternal flames of hell, but instead they most OFTEN answer, "Look, I've got my own —. I was born a ——-, I was raised a ——-, and I'm going to die a ——-!" Most of them might as well have added, "And I'm going to go to hell a ——!" Church membership does NOT give a person entrance into the Kingdom of God but only by being born again, as Jesus declares in John 3:3-5, and Revelation 3:20, where He tells us how. "I'm standing at the door of your life and I'm knocking. If you will invite Me to come in to your life and heart as Saviour King of everything, then I will come in." That's how to be born again!

But after we're born again it's VERY important that we don't begin making excuses for not measuring up to God's will for us, because contrary to what we may have been taught, there is no excuse for not doing the will of God! I've often wondered what would have happened in the Garden of Eden if Adam would not have tried to make excuses, when God came and asked him why he "messed up". Instead, Adam said, "The woman!" (Then he added), "Whom

YOU GAVE to me..." I wonder what would have happened if Adam would have said, "Lord, please don't blame Eve. Let all the blame be upon me. She's the weaker vessel, and I should have been looking out for her." Or what if Eve would have said the same. Instead she blamed the serpent. The only good thing I can think of to say about the devil is that when God came to him, he didn't pass the buck, or or try to place blame. (Never mind the fact that he didn't have any place to pass it!)

But it is impossible for us to be both EXCUSING and REPENTING at the same time. Besides, God will NOT forgive what we are excusing. Most Christians have been brainwashed, hypnotized or otherwise programmed into thinking that "nobody's perfect". They even use this kind of reasoning as an excuse for sinning in the first place and for not repenting in the second place. The excuse, "I'm only human after all,..." is typical, but definitely counterproductive. Remember, the Lord gives, in His Word, many victory promises: I Corinthians 10:13 says that, "There has NO temptation taken you but such as is common to man: but GOD IS FAITHFUL, Who will NOT let you be tempted above what you are able, but will with the temptation also make a way to escape that you may be able to bear it." And in II Corinthians 2:14, "Now thanks be unto God, who ALWAYS causes us to TRIUMPH IN CHRIST, and makes manifest the savour of His knowledge by us in every place." (Victory—Always—everywhere!!!) And Romans 8:37, "...In ALL THESE THINGS WE ARE MORE THAN CONQUERORS THROUGH HIM that

56

loved (s) us!" And, Philippians 4:13, "I can do ALL things through Christ who strengthens me!!!"

But, so many of us, if we were honest and consistent with our own system of unbelief and wrong doctrine, have CHANGED these very victory Scriptures to read OTHER THAN what God has actually said!!!! We have tended to say "NO! God has NOT given me a way to escape!" or "NO! God does NOT cause me to triumph in every place and circumstance!" or "NO! I am NOT more than a conqueror in all or even very many of these things!" "I am not even a conqueror, much less, more than a conqueror."

A QUICK BUT PERHAPS NECESSARY LOOK AT A WRONG DOCTRINE

Intricately interwoven into the fabric of our thinking is some wrong doctrine that has been "bee-ing" spuriously spread throughout nearly all of Christendom. Protestants and Catholics, EVERY denomination — it seems that hardly anyone has been spared. This doctrine of the dualism of nature, concerns our attitude toward our bodies, toward pleasure, our flesh, perfection, victory, — towards Life itself! A fresh revelation realization of The King's Greatest Secret changes all this.

MONSTROUS MANICHEAN MADNESS

The Church was fully free of faulty thinking in this area until about the fourth and fifth century after Christ, when a funny but phoney philosophy of "dualism" infiltrated the Church from a man called "the father of Christian philosophy and theology". He introduced a warped way of thinking into the Church that was not corrected by the theologians or philosophers that were to follow. Here is the man, the doctrine and the correction to his approach.

St Augustine, 354-430 A.D. was a Greek Manicheist philosopher prior to his coming into the Church. Here, we quote from the World Book Dictionary, "Manichean (man' e ke" en), a member of a Gnostic sect, arising in Persia in the 200's A.D., compounded of Christian, Buddhistic, Zoroastrian, and other beliefs, and maintaining a theological dualism in which the body and matter were identified with darkness and evil, and the soul, striving to liberate itself, was identified with light and goodness." In other words, while the Hebrews believed matter and the body to be bad or good, depending upon the use to which it was put, - the Manichiests believed, and taught that the body was evil, and that every thing that the body did, or was, or said, was only always exceedingly sinful. Sound familiar? Nearly every church and catechism and liturgy we know of has something of this within it. Some have even given the illustration that inside every person there is a white dog nature and a black dog nature and that the one that wins is the one you say "sic 'em" to (or feed) the most. That's what we mean by "dualism".

The Hebrews said that matter, a pen, a human body was not bad in itself, but that its goodness or badness was determined by what one did with that matter or pen or human body. This is why, in Romans, Paul says that "the instruments of our body are slaves of righteousness if we yield them to do righteous things, and that they are instruments of unrighteousness if we yield them to do unrighteous things."

But the manicheans said that our body members are bad, because they were made of substance, of material, of matter. So in Augustine's writings, he says that it is a sin to watch a dog chase a rabbit. Why? Because the body gets excited and involved, and says, "Let's see now, is the dog gonna catch the rabbit, or is the rabbit gonna catch the dog!" Augustine said, "I have learned to take my food as medicine." In other words, he disciplined himself to the place where a big juicy piece of beefsteak tasted like cod liver oil, just so his body would not get all involved, excited, and sinful. My well rounded mother told me one time that every act of sex was sinful. (She had four grown children!) She quoted David's verse, "I was born and conceived in sin." She didn't know the Jewish tradition about David's personal family situation. I said, "Mother, what a terrible thing to say about us kids." (We discuss this more fully in our book, THE SEXUAL MINISTRY, available at Great Commission Ministries, P.O. 7123, Mpls., MN., 55407. Love Offerings, to help provide for this and other books and Bibles for others, are tax deductible.)

The real question is NOT "Can I keep from sinning?" but "Is God great enough to keep me from sinning?!." Is He? If someone asks me, "Do you ever get a wrong spirit or attitude toward your wife or children or anyone?" or if they say, "Don't you ever sin?" I respond, "I don't recommend it!" or "We're not in favor of it." If they argue, "Do you actually think a person can get through the day without sinning!?" I respond, "We'd advise it."

Mark Twain allegedly wrote in his memoirs, "Went to church today. Preacher preached on sin. Only problem was, I couldn't rahtly tell whether he was for it, 'r again' it!" You know? Sometimes a body cain't tell by looking at some Christians' lives and doctrines whether or not they're in favor of sin or against it either!!!

HOW LONG CAN YOU LIVE
WITHOUT SINNING?

I John 1:9 says that "If we confess our sins, God is faithful and just, ...and will cleanse us from - (not much, or most, but) - ALL unrighteousness!!!" Let's say you just "I John 1:9'ed" it. How much unrighteousness do you got left in yuh? Doesn't it say cleansed from ALL?!. How long can you stay cleansed from all unrighteousness through the power of God, and by the Strength, and through the Life of God lived through you??? 5 seconds? 5 minutes, by God your Strength? 5 hours, through Christ your Power? 5 days, with Christ as your Life? 5 decades, with Jesus Christ AS YOUR RIGHTEOUSNESS!!!!!?!. (Please refer to the above list of Scriptures here. Or would you rather continue on in your excuse making and cannibalizing?)

IF GOD DIDN'T MAKE LITTLE GREEN
APPLES IN MINNEAPOLIS

Paul, in Philippians 3, uses the word 'perfect' in two different ways. In verse 12 he says he's not perfect and

60

in verse 15 he says that he IS!!! (I wonder why we only always hear that he's not?) Imagine, if you will, a little green apple, just barely past the blossom stage, a little bitty nubbin of a thing. But it's perfect! No worms, germs, dust, crust, must or rust. It's not dashed, bashed, crashed, slashed, hashed or gnashed. And now, can you picture a perfectly perfect apple that's ruby, rudy, rosy, red, ripe and juicy? If it were any more ripe, it would be rotten; and if it were any less ripe it would be sour and woody. Please ask yourself this question: What particular things are necessary for a smaller apple's growth and development into this mature apple? Are bruises, or worms or rot necessary? Is "hanging in there" necessary? — To endure the long cold nights? the hot summer days, the wind, and rain?

Some folks seem to think that rebellion, back-slidings, detours, lapses, wrong attitudes and spastic silliness are all necessary to our growth and development in God.

There IS a discipline, but it is a discipline that pertains to the new person or new man in Christ Jesus, and not the old man or old self or nature. The old life HAS BEEN crucified with Christ — not "is being". We don't believe in beating the dead carcass. That would be wasted effort, and futile. (Ro.6)

So, we see that the flesh is NEITHER good nor bad in or of itself, BUT depending upon the use to which it is put. Adam, before he fell, had flesh, and our redeemed bodies will be flesh. Even Jesus had flesh! Hebrews 5 speaks of Jesus, "Who in the days of His flesh...offered up prayers with strong crying and

61

tears...and...though He were a Son, yet learned He obedience through the things which He suffered. And BEING MADE PERFECT, He became the Author of eternal salvation unto all them that obey Him." Wasn't Jesus already perfect? Of course! But here we see that He also needed to "become perfect"! Can we be perfect in the I John 1:9 "cleansed from ALL unrighteousness" sense? Of course, but we also need to become perfect in the "ripe apple" sense of "growing in grace and in the knowledge of the Son of God" and in the sense of Paul's pressing "toward the mark for the prize of the high calling of God in Christ Jesus" - the fulfillment of our adventures and destinies and callings of God!!!

CRISIS AND PROCESS

So, there is both a crisis and a process to every experience that we are to have in God: the new birth, the Lordship of Christ, Sanctification, (dedicated and made holy), the Holy Spirit, etc.

Ask some "Christians" if they are saved, and they'll say, "I dunno, I'm workin' on it." (The Bible says we can KNOW! I Jn.5). But because they are always "working on" the process of salvation, without the CRISIS of having been born again, they won't be...., because they are always GOING THROUGH the door, but never quite get IN. But then you ask others if they're saved, and they say, "Ya sure, I got saved 90 years ago!" But too many of them got saved and stuck! They got through the door and then went to sleep for 89 years. The same thing is true of the Holy Spirit. Some believe only in the process of being filled while others got "it", and got stuck, (or sprung leaks!). And the same thing is true with The King's Greatest Secret — BOTH the crisis of appropriation AND the process of abiding in Him - moment by moment, both are necessary.

ARE YOU NOW READY TO DIE THEN LIVE!!!

You simply: # 1. Know and "RECKON YOUR-SELF TO HAVE BEEN CRUCIFIED WITH CHRIST" (Rom.6:6 — this is the crisis), and # 2. THEN "CONSIDER AND RECKON YOUR-SELF (here is the process) AS DEAD INDEED UNTO SIN, SELF AND satan, but alive unto God through Jesus Christ our Lord!!! (Rom.6:11) ALLELUJAHWEH!!!

Thank you, Dear Lord Jesus, for taking us to the cross with You and for raising us up with You in newness of Life in You. Lord God, we receive You to BE all that You are, in us, now and forever more. We receive You AS OUR VERY LIFE to BE OUR VERY LIFE!!! Please now, LIVE YOUR VERY LIFE THROUGH ME!!! In Jesus' Name. Amen.

Jesus said, "BE YE THEREFORE PERFECT, EVEN AS YOUR FATHER IN HEAVEN IS PERFECT." Matt. 5:48. Jesus, as always, meant just what He said! He meant "BE as perfect as God!" Or would you prostitute and change and twist and warp and non-effectualize the Word of God here or any other place?

It does NOT mean: "try to be perfect", nor "be perfect sometime after your body has rotted", nor "give up on being perfect", nor "it's impossible to be perfect", nor "wish that you were perfect", nor "God isn't great enough to make or keep me perfect", nor "be theoretically (or "pretend") perfect", nor any of that kind of silliness. "Would be" disciples of the Kingdom, WON'T BE disciples of the Kingdom of God as long as they are messing with the commands of the King of God's Kingdom in this way! One who changes the commands of the King is a Kingdom anarchist and traitor. When someone asks, "What does this Verse mean?" the best answer always is, "The Bible—this Verse—means just what it says!" because the King means what He says. I believe that whenever there is a disagreement about a Scripture, it is because one or more of them is not willing to accept what the Scripture and King says.

THE GREATEST MOMENT OF MY LIFE

One day Patty Troug at Bethel College told me, "John, as long as you are calling 'idealistic', 'unattainable', or 'theoretical' what God calls 'necessary', 'practical','available', and 'attainable', YOU are calling God a LIAR!!!" I had thrown a book away from me in disgust, *FOREVER TRIUMPHANT*, by Huegel, in which he quoted II Corinthians 2:14, "Thanks be unto God who in Christ ALWAYS causes us to triumph and manifests Christ through us in EVERY place!" (JB) "Victory, at ALL times and in every place!" I had said "that's too idealistic", but then I realized, as a result of Patricia's gentle rebuke, that I had been calling God a liar in that He had said, "Victory always and everywhere." And I had said,

64

"Impossible". I did not want to call God a liar anymore, so I went to my room, got out my Bibles, KJV, AMP, Gdspd, Greek N.T., etc., and laid them out on Bruce Leafblad's vacant bunk, and got down on my knees in order to see just what God DID say. Sure enough, God said, "Perfect victory always" AND "More than conquerors" AND "Abundant Life" AND "Joy unspeakable" AND "Full of Glory" AND "WE have the Mind of Christ" AND "Christ our Life" AND "whatever we ask" AND "Greater works than these shall ye do" AND "I can do all things through Christ" AND "With God all things are possible" etc., etc., etc., etc. All these Bibles said the same thing!! So, I decided to do three things:

1. Confess every known sin, including having called God a liar;

2. Yield COMPLETELY to the Lord Jesus Christ. I told the Lord Jesus that I would be willing to be sick, maimed, killed, single, celibate, persecuted, misunderstood, forgotten, married to anyone He said (I was sure He was going to make me marry somebody really terrible). Anyway, I really meant business.

Now, these first two steps I had taken many times before, but I took them again. In fact, we should always keep up to date with the Lord, staying free from sin and staying in a totally yielded state.

3. Appropriate by faith the highest level walk in God's Spirit, with Christ AS our Life! Invite Jesus Christ to come in to our life, and actually BE our life

and to LIVE HIS LIFE through us, and take over completely as Saviour, Lord and Life!!!

Charles Trumble, in *The Life That Wins,* says that on this third step of faith, everything now depends. He suggested that we take a step of faith with total disregard for the presence (or lack of), accompanying signs or proofs, because the transaction must be based on faith rather than some feeling or tingle, etc. So, I remember reaching out my hand to the Lord God and saying, "Lord Jesus, I believe You have a walk for me that I haven't been experiencing; a relationship and an experience with You that I haven't had before. Lord Jesus, I don't know what to call it, and I don't know how to get it, but whatever You call it and however one gets it, I receive it from You now in cold, blind faith, not depending on outward feelings or 'signs' as the proof of the transaction. Thank You very much. In Jesus' Name, Amen."

Can you guess what happened? You guessed it. Nothing. Outwardly, or on a feeling level, that is. I felt really dead. Oh, I had accepted the Lord Jesus as my personal Saviour many years before, and I had yielded my Life to Him many times before. But the same thing had happened to me as would have happened in the Old Testament if one would have taken a clean lamb of the flock without blemish and then sacrificed the lamb under the hot Israel sun...and that's all. Can you imagine the mess? The sacrifice NEEDED the fire of God to come from heaven to light upon and consume the sacrifice as a sign of acceptance and anointing. But I rose from my knees there at Gerald Healy's house where Bruce Leafblad and I were roommates while attending Bethel College, November 1960, my senior year. I put away all my Bibles and climbed wearily into my top bunk. After I was settled down, I thought, "If anybody asked me to praise the Lord right now, it would be like someone asking me to praise a haystack." I suppose I was remembering a time when I had gone to visit a church and had tried to get "ba'tahzd wi' d' HoliGoz'" and the pastor was on one side telling me to say "Pah-rayz Gawd" just as loud as I could, whilst the preacher's wife was on the other side, encouraging me to say, "How'lay-lew'yuh" just as fast as I could. I recall how terribly difficult it had been to say either one either way. Folks who know me now are surprised that I didn't bound out of my mother's womb shouting "How'lay-lew'ya". One time, at Bible School, a staff member said the reason John Bohlen praised the Lord was because he had a 'sanguine' personality. I told her, "Yes, Joyce, the 47th Psalm says, 'O clap your hands, [all ye SANGUINES], shout unto God with the voice of triumph'!!!'" By the way, that's not quite how it reads—it reads 'ALL YE PEOPLE'. So it's not just those with an enthusiastic personality that are to beautifully and enthusiastically and constantly worship the Lord: ALL of us are.

CATACLYSMIC REVOLUTION

Anyway, no sooner had that thought crossed my mind about praising a haystack, (indicating the lacking emotional level of positive feeling) when Christ BECAME my Life!, and I have never been the same since! It seemed like a great dam broke on the inside and there came explosively gushing over me, and through me, and to me, and from me, and upon me, and around me, from deep within and from high above came the Glory of God, and the Joy of God, and the Love of God, and the Spirit of God, and the LIFE of God, and the Peace of God, and the Presence of God, and the Strength of God, and the Anointing of God, and the Effervescent Flooding Overflowing Fullness of the Living God!!! I have never been the same! Fabulous! Incredible! Joyful! Invigorating! Beautiful! Astounding! Healing! Wonderful! Marvelous! Lasting! Satisfying! Miraculous! Life-changing! Christ BECAME my Life! I saw myself as having been crucified with Christ, dead and buried with Christ, RISEN AND REIGNING WITH CHRIST JESUS in newness of Life, and seated IN Christ AT the Father's right hand, far over and above EVERYTHING that is named in heaven and on earth, and GLORIFIED IN HIM - Jesus Christ! This is described in Eph. 2, and Col. 3, Rom. 6, and Rom. 8, Eph. 3, II Cor. 3, etc., etc., etc. (Time out - for a Glory Spell and a happy dance! Would you like to dance with me?!)

Note: From the Amplified Bible, Eph. 3:19b - "That you may be filled (through all your being) unto all the fullness of God - [that is], may have the RICHEST measure of the Divine Presence, and become a body WHOLLY filled and flooded with God Himself." Peter says, "Having become PARTAKERS OF THE DIVINE NATURE" and Colossians says, "When CHRIST Who IS OUR LIFE - - -" and "For in Him the whole fullness of Deity (the Godhead), continues to dwell in bodily form - giving complete expression of the Divine Nature. And you are IN HIM, made FULL, and have come to fullness of life - in Christ YOU TOO are FILLED with the GODHEAD: Father, Son and the Holy Spirit, and reach full spiritual stature - - -!!!" (Amp)

The question for all of us, no matter what our theological back-ground is: Are you FILLED WITH GOD RIGHT NOW? Jesus said, "He that believes in Me, out of his innermost being shall gush forth flooding torrents of Living Water continuously." Talkin' 'bout you?

Question—Are you full of God and His Holy Spirit right this moment? Are you up to date with Him and on excellent terms with Him right now? Do you minister and share from the overflow, or are you like a "small handful of water in a big empty barrel." Pray with me?....

Dear Father God, thank You for providing unlimited anointing and every blessing, and having "given us all things that pertain to life and godliness". I ask You to BE my life; be ALL that You ARE, in me from now on. I reckon and consider my old life to be dead. I receive You AS my "Wisdom, Righteousness, Sanctification, and Redemption". BE my Perfection, Love through me, speak Your Words Through me, pray through me. Thank You, Mighty-Right-Now God. I believe from now on that I can do ALL things through Christ my Life, and that nothing shall be impossible IN YOU. In Jesus' Name. Amen.

There is a true story of a little boy who was looking intently into the baptistry after the baptism service, when his mother came up and asked him what he was doing. He said, "I'm looking for that 'old man' the pastor said we left in the water!" You see, this is the true meaning of baptism by immersion - our total identification with Christ in His crucifixion, death, burial, resurrection, ascension and glorification.

THE THIRD COMING OF CHRIST?!?!!.

Assume with me for a moment that God wants to return to the earth in a THIRD way. He came as a Babe, and He's coming in the clouds. But pretend with me, that between His 1st and 2nd Coming, He wants to come in a 3rd way. Imagine that this time, He wants to come disguised as a regular person, and that He wants to do it like this. Suppose someone is sitting in church, and has a cardiac attack, and dies, God forbid. Instead of rushing to give the person artificial recuperation, the rest of the people, if they notice at all, think that that person just fell asleep for a minute. Suppose that before anyone else knows of this, Christ comes in to this person, blinks open his eyes, and starts walking around in his shoes in disguise, incognito, speaking, talking, loving, LIVING, His LIFE, - - - the very LIFE of Christ Himself!

He wants to be glorified and magnified now IN all who believe!! Notice this Scripture! "When He shall come to be glorified IN His saints and to be admired IN all them that believe, (because our testimony among you was believed) in that day" II Th. 1:10.

70

"Christ IN YOU, THE HOPE OF GLORY!!!" Colossians 1:28. The KJV calls it "the MYSTERY which hath been hid from ages and from generations, but NOW is made manifest to His saints! To whom God would make known THE RICHES OF THE GLORY OF THIS MYSTERY AMONG THE GENTILES, WHICH IS - - - **CHRIST IN YOU,** THE HOPE OF GLORY!!!"

The Williams translation calls this God's Glorious "OPEN SECRET — CHRIST IN YOU!!!" and Beck's Translation calls it "THE GLORY OF THIS HIDDEN TRUTH — CHRIST IN YOU!!!" I have called this, THE KING'S GREATEST SECRET!!!!!!!!!!! Please dear Dear One, please do NOT let this truth pass you by... Please stay with this until this truth becomes nitty gritty gut-level REALITY IN YOUR HEART! IN JESUS' Name. Amen.

So, back to the illustration - Say that Christ came into your available dead body and BECAAAAAAAA-AAAAAAAAAAAME it's Life, that is, started living His Glorious Life THROUGH you, loving THROUGH you, loving, talking, loving, walking, loving, living, loving, blessing, loving, healing, loving, BEING ALL THAT HE IS - IN YOU, - BEING your Salvation, NOT giving you Salvation as an experience APART from Him, but living it, BE-ing, it DO-ing it through you!!

I Corinthians 1:30 says that Christ, "IS MADE unto us Wisdom, and Righteousness, and Sanctification, and Redemption". These things: Resurrection, Salvation, etc., are not a "thing", or an "experience" apart from Him, but are a PERSON. That Person's

Name is YAHWEH YAHSHUA, The Mighty Right Now God, The Lord and Saviour Jesus Christ!!! Even in the Old Testament, please notice all of the times it refers to Yahweh as BEING our Sword, our Shield, our Fortress, our Buckler, our Exceeding Great Reward, our High Tower "I will run into Him and be safe"!!! Not "gives us a sword" but "IS MY SWORD"!!! Dear Heart, please - can you see the difference???

Some people come staggering into church on Sunday morning to get their weakly injection fix of righteousness to last them barely till next Sunday, but Jesus wants to BE our Righteousness!!! BE our LIFE, our Salvation and Protection. Salvation is not a "thing". Salvation is a Person! And His Name is Jesus Christ! As I John says, "He that hath the Son hath LIFE and he that hath not the Son of God hath not life."

INFERIORITY COMPLEX

They tell about a man who was down at the altar praying, "Lord, show me I'm nothing, show me I'm nothing." Then the preacher came along and said, "Take it by faith, brother." I used to have a terrible bad inferiority complex. Then somebody came along and told me I didn't have a 'feriority complex - I was just PLAIN INFERIOR!!! I used to do things constantly to "compensate" for my deep seated feelings of inadequacy. The ol' one room country school we went to was called "Wild Cat School". Then we went into town to the citified junior high school, and, truth to tell, I didn't rightly know how to

73

act around all those city-wise kids. So, to try to do something about my 9th grade inferiority complex, I thought maybe I could get a book from the school lie-berry. The first book I got said,........ "Act natural!" But that didn't help much, you see, 'cause the thing that I "naturally" was, I knew I couldn't afford to publicly be!

So, I got another book,..... an' it said,..... "Be yourself." But that didn't help either, because MY old self definitely WAS inferior! Later on, my friend, Lee Eliason, told me to "be sincere", and that helped some, but here, as a senior at Bethel College, my discovery of this Greatest Secret fully met the needs of my life along this line because Christ BECAME my sufficiency and my adequacy!!!!!!!! This really Really REALLY solved the problem!!!

So you don't need to die or commit suicide - because Christ wants to become your LIFE by your acceptance. Accept what He did when He took NOT ONLY our sins and sicknesses, so we can be forgiven and healed completely, but He took our SELVES. (Rom. 6, Col, Eph., etc.) He put US to death with ALL of our insufficiencies, inadequacies, inferiorities, inabilities, instabilities, everything negative, nasty, weak and sinful, and took us to the cross, put us to death, buried us and raised us up in newness of life, a whole new, beautiful, glorious, adequate, sufficient, wonderful, able, stable creation fashioned in His image, that He wants to actually BEEEEEEEEEE the Life of!!!!!!!!!

THE ELEPHANT AND THE FLEA

The story is told of an elephant that had a friend who was a flea that rode around behind his ear. They used to have lots of happy times together. One day they crossed a jungle bridge that shook, and swung and swayed. After crossing the bridge, the flea whispered into his friend's, (the elephant's) ear. Said the tiny little flea, "We sure shook that bridge didn't we!!" And at the end of each of your days, you can whisper into the Ear of your Friend, Yahweh, your Creator King, "We sure shook our world today, didn't we?" Jesus wants to beeeeeeeee your LIFE!!!!!!!!!!!!!!!!

A BEE IN YOUR BONNET

Did you know that Christ is NOT interested in HELPING you to be righteous, or wise, or strong, or alive, apart or distant from Himself?? He wants to BEEEEEEE your Righteousness, BEEEE your Wisdom, BEEEEEEE your Strength, BEEEEEEEEE your Life, BEEEEE your Everything. He doesn't want to HELP you say good words, or pray, or be disciplined, or heal, or bless, or love, as something distinct, distant, or apart from Himself. He wants to pray His prayers through you by the Holy Spirit, to say His words through you, to bless with His blessing through you, to Heal with His Healing through you, to love with His love through you. Christ wants to BEEEEEEEEEEEE all that He is, on location, through you!!! Do you see the difference? Do you?

THE GLORY SPELL

I was counselling with a 70 year old woman who had problems. She had a "glory spell" when I told her about the King's Greatest Secret! She said, "I was born again and baptized in the Holy Spirit when I was 10 years old and have been walking close to God ever since. But in all the 60 years I've walked with God, I've never once heard these truths, that Christ can actually BEEEEE my LIFE!!" When a person truly comes to know this wonderful Secret, then the transformation in a person's life should be just as great as if Christ Himself actually BECAAAME that person's very LIFE!!! Interested?! Interested in sharing this Secret? Interested in helping us share this Secret?!

It has been tremendously exciting to share the King's Greatest Secret with so many dear ones. As of today, over 24,000 copies of this chapter have been distributed around the world, by means of our 1st book, *How To Rule The World,* or *Seek 1st The Kingdom Of God!* As of this printing, another 35,000 copies of the chapter will be available through, not only Rule The World, but also through our book on marriage called, The Sexual Ministry, our book on the family called, How To Raise "Purfect" Kids, and also this book!!! We also want to make available a booklet called "The King's Greatest Secret", and we already have a 90 minute cassette tape available by the same title. If you would like these materials, or want to help us "get the word out" with your tax deductible contributions, please write: The Great Commission Ministries, Box 7123, Mpls., MN 55407.

A FOUNDATION STONE!

This Secret is so very very foundational to virtually every other truth in Scripture. For example, with regard to prayer, we must believe for Christ Himself to be on location, praying His prayers through us, according to the will of the Heavenly Father, by the power of the Holy Spirit. With regard to miracles or a ministry, we are to believe that Christ is on location, ministering and BEING that ministry through us.

So, we can have an experience GREATER THAN if we had a heart attack and Jesus Christ came into our newly dead body and started living in the earth disguised AS US, because better than this CAN BE OURS by accepting that we were crucified with Christ already on the cross in order for Him to LIVE HIS LIFE IN AND THROUGH US!!! Now He wants to BE all that He is in us, BE our life, etc. If Jesus IS our righteousness, we'll be as righteous as the Father, because Jesus is as righteous as the Father!!! Remember Jesus said in Matthew 5:48 - "BE YE THEREFORE PERFECT EVEN AS YOUR FATHER IN HEAVEN IS PERFECT." That's how we do it. Simply reckon the old life to be dead (Rom. 6), and receive Christ, not only inside to BE your Saviour and Master and total Lord, but also BEING all that He is, in you, as your Life!!! Are you ready?!!!!!!

HE wants to walk around in YOUR shoes, wearing YOUR clothes, speaking HIS words, praying HIS prayers, thinking HIS thoughts, blessing HIS people, loving, healing through you. He wants to BE the Parent of your children, the Spouse of your mate, the Worker on your job, the Child of your parents, the Friend of your friends, the Leader in your church, the Leader in your community, the Changer of your world, the Establisher of His Kingdom, the Binder and Looser of situations, the Fulfiller of the Great Commission and ALL His commandments, IN YOU and THROUGH YOU!!! (Matt 28:18-20, I John 2). ALL THIS CAN BE YOURS FROM NOW ON as CHRIST IS YOUR LIFE!! (I John 4:17). AMEN!!!!!!!

Christ wants there to be NO DIFFERENCE between who He is at the right hand of the Father and who He is - IN US!!!!! Amen!!!

If you have any question about this, leave no stone unturned until you know deeeeeeeeeeep within your heart - - - this Greatest Secret of the King, if you can't get the Secret any other way please get in touch with us - because this MUST become absolutely clear to you, absolutely workable! It's the Key literally to EVERYTHING you are in God.

Instead of a crucifix, I've often thought of having a cross with nothing on it except a mirror, as a reminder that you were "there when they crucified my Lord"! And when He rose up from the grave!!!

Here it is then - God's Greatest Secret!!! Christ living His Glorified Life in you AS your Life!!! CHRIST LIVING HIS GLORIFIED LIFE IN YOU -IN ME - AS OUR GLORIFIED LIFE!!! This chapter - this concept - these truths - are the most important thing in this book! If I only have one chance to tell people one thing, I tell them this. The vast majority of Christians, (I would say more than 99%), do not have a working knowledge of this Greatest Secret of God. I believe that the need is so great for people to know this truth, that if you and I dedicated the rest of our entire lives to sharing this one truth, it would be worth while! What is your life being dedicated to at the present time anyway? If you are interested, let us know, or if you want a tape or the book, *How To Rule The World,* or *Seek 1st The Kingdom Of God,* that amplifies this truth, on "The King's Greatest Secret", or if you want to contribute to the cause, write K.O.G., P.O. 7123, Mpls., MN., 55407. Or if you want to help get this message to others, make a tax deductible check out to "the Kingdom of God" or Great Commission Ministries and send it to us. Let's make sure that this Secret, remains a "secret" no longer!

What would happen if Christ came to the earth to live in disguise in someone before His coming in the clouds? What if He came to live His glorified Life in Your town? Your family? Your church? Your factory? Your marriage? Your shoes? Well, that's exactly what Christ wants to happen!!! Exactly! NO DIFFERENCE.

Please now let us make a prayer by amplifying of II Thessalonians 1:10,

"Lord God of the impossible, now and forever, please now come and be made all glorious in me and be marvelled at in me. I believe Lord God, I believe, for You to live Your life - IN ME. Yea, BE my Life! I reckon my old life to be crucified! dead! and buried! I consider my New Life to be risen! Ascended! Seated! Glorified! and Reigning! In You, and You in me — Right Now! In THIS world! In MY life! As My Life! FROM NOW ON! And to tell this Secret to as many as possible! As quickly as possible! By whatever means possible! In as many places as possible! In

Jesus Name, Amen!! "AS CHRIST IS — SO ARE WE — IN THIS WORLD ! ! !"

Who would dare to put an upper limit on the marvelous possibilities of this spectacular truth!, this "Mystery of the Gospel of the Ages!, this King's Greatest Secret!?

In the Mighty Name of Yahweh Yahshua, Jesus Christ the Righteous, we insist that this Truth not be limited! Look at the above list of Scriptures again. Here are only a few in closing: 1. "I can do ALL things through Christ Who strengthens me!" (Ph.4:13) 2. "We...are transformed into God's very same image!!!" (II Co.3:18) 3. "The works that I do shall you do, and greater works than these shall ye do!!" (John 14) 4. "Even as He walks!!" (I John 2:6) 5. "AS HE IS — SO ARE WE — IN THIS WORLD!!!!!" (I John 4:17)

Now, let's look at one of the things that might happen if your friend learns this Secret.

CHAPTER THREE — REVIEW

1. Is it possible to live without sinning? (Explain).
2. What of ours did Christ take with Him to the cross?
3. What is God's greatest secret?
4. What is the difference between Christ helping you do or speak good things & Him speaking or doing good things through you?
5. Why was it necessary for Christ to take you with Him to the cross?
6. Without a practical revelation understanding of the King's Greatest Secret, has positive thinking got much power?
7. Why is suicide not necessary?
8. The following phrases go with what Scripture verses (you may look them up from the list of Scriptures provided below):

   Victory _____, Victory always everywhere _____ , Free from sin _____ , Risen with Christ our life _____ , Seated in Christ _____ , Fullness of joy: joy unspeakable _____ , Every blessing _____ , Joy of the Lord - strength _____ , Mind of Christ _____ , Can do all things through Christ _____ , Walk blamelessly _____ , All power and authority _____ , We are the light of the World _____ , To live is Christ _____ , All power and authority _____ ,

What ever we ask _____ , Abundant Life
_____ , We have all things for life
_____ , More than conquerors _____ ,
We can be as He is all things are possible
_____ , We can walk as He walked
_____ , Greater works _____ , We can
know the mysteries of the Gospel of the ages,
Christ is made unto us, Wisdom .

Jude 24; Ph. 1:21; Eph. 1:3,4; Rom. 8:37; Col.
3:1-3; II Cor.2:14-16; Matt. 5:14; II Pet. 1:1-4;
John 14:13; Ps. 16:11; Rom. 6:7,18,22; Ph. 4:13;
Ne. 8:10; Eph. 2:6; I Cor. 15:57; Cor. 2:16; Matt.
28:18; II Cor. 9:8; I Cor. 1:30; Luke 8:10; I John
4:17; John 10:10; John 14:12; Mat. 19:26; Col.
1:25-29; I John 2:6.

9. Gal.2:20 - Are you living?
10. Can we be perfect?
11. What did Jesus mean when He said, "Be
    perfect !"? (Matt.5:48).
12. How can we be perfect?
13. What is the main solution for most arguments
    about the Bible?
14. How is "calling 'idealistic' what God calls
    necessary and practical" - calling God a liar?
15. What 3 steps are necessary for Christ to be your
    Life?
16. Do you have the mind of Christ?
17. In the Word, what's the main evidence, sign, fruit,
    or proof that you are full of God?
18. Not "have" you been filled with, but are you full
    of God right now? (Give yourself a percentage)

82

19. What would happen to a clean and freshly sacrificed (killed) lamb under the hot Israel sun if nothing more happened after it was killed?
20. What else is necessary?
21. What is this symbolic of?
22. Who should praise the Lord with shouting & clapping? (Ps.47).
23. Why can we have an experience MORE REAL than if we fell dead and Christ was looking around for a fresh warm dead body He could move into and raise up and become the Life of, living on the earth again - disguised as you?
24. Who is the flea - the elephant in the illustration?
25. What is the main difference between Christ helping us do or be something, and Him being or doing it in and through us?
26. Are we suposed to discipline the old nature or the old self?
27. Does Christ want there to be any difference between who He is at the Father's right hand & who He is — in us?
28. If you devoted the rest of your live to sharing this Secret — would your life be well spent?
29. Will you?

CHAPTER 4 — OUTLINE

WHEN DID I TOUCH THE KING?

I. The "Hog Waller"
II. Touch The King
III. Selected Scriptures on Kingdom Anarchy
IV. Accredited To Your Account
V. Kingdom Anarchy—Some Examples
    A. The Messenger Boy
    B. The Afternoon Snack
    C. The Hunter
VI. Review

WHEN DID I TOUCH THE KING?
or
ARE YOU A HAWG WALLER WALLERER?
or
DO YOU LIKE HAWG WALLERS?
or
KINGDOM ANARCHY, SEDITION, AND INSURRECTION

DEAR READER,

I felt that both the last chapter on the King's Greatest Secret and also that this chapter and the next was so important to the message in this book that I have taken the liberty to include these three chapters from my book How To Rule The World. While some of you may be frustrated with me about this, (and to those of you who are, I humbly apologize), nevertheless, there may be many dear ones who have never read our other books that will only get a chance to read from the material presented here. Thank you for being patient with me in this "foolishness of preaching"!!! Some may also object to my use of "country talk" or slang, and some of you, no doubt, can say it better. Please take the liberty to do so, in your talking and teaching about these things.

THE HOG WALLER

One day, while interceding for Minneapolis and St. Paul, I received a "visionette" which I believe is from the Lord. You will be able to picture it with me. I could see two hills beside one another with a tree in the foreground and a path coming down off the hill past a "hog-waller" by the tree. Do you know what a hog-waller is? Well, a hog-waller is a mud hole what hogs like to "waller" in. Well, down this here path come, guess what? You guessed it. A hawg! And can you guess what this here PURTY pink hog did when it got to the mud hole? You guessed it! Jumped right in, he did (I think it was a he. A feller wouldn't hardly think a lady gender would like hog-wallers that much). Well, just about that time a be-you-too-full, fluffy, snow white kitty cat come a tippy toein' it down the path, and can you guess what that there cat done when it got to the mud hole? Well, believe it or not, that cat jumped scat into that mud hole and started to havin' a happy time. Next, down the path come a Be-you-too-full little baby lamb, whose fleece was white as snow, Lo, behold and consternation, (I wonder how you guessed it?), that there little, peer white lamb jumped in that hog-waller and started to havin' a happy time. Why from the way it was actin' you'da thunk it was a mutton head!

I asked the Lord, "Lord, what are You trying to show me?" And it seemed as though the Lord said, "The mud hole represents anarchy of the Kingdom of God, or Kingdom rebellion, sedition, mutiny, anarchy, treachery, insurrection, treason, insubordination, stubbornness, etc. The pig represents natural man, with his natural propensity for such things; the kitten represents religious man; and the lamb represents spiritual people." Whereupon I said, "Yes, but it's against the nature of a kitten and a lamb to like mud." It seemed as though the Lord said "It's also contrary to the nature of spiritual and religious people to like rebellion, anarchy, sedition, mutiny, treachery, insurrection, insubordination, treason, and stubbornness." Then it seemed as though the Lord Jesus began to show me what He has been putting up with. I could visualize a person with his hand stretched to the Lord, saying, "Lord Jesus, I love You, but I refuse to accept this one whom You send," or, "I love You God, but I'll not accept what You have to say to me through this one or that one."

The definition of Kingdom anarchy or an anarchist is: "Any ONE or any THING that rejects or fails to cooperate with anyone the King sends or anything that the King directs or desires."

WHEN DID I TOUCH THE KING

Remember the story of the excited woman who had been promised a visit at her house from the King in person? When only a child, a poor beggar and an old man appeared during that day, she was disappointed and next day asked the King why He did not come. He said, "I did come, but I was disguised as a child, a poor beggar, and an old man; and do you remember how you received Me?"

Chris Wold Dyrud

SELECTED SCRIPTURES ON
KINGDOM ANARCHY

Consider the following Scriptural examples of Kingdom Anarchy:

1. Matt. 10:40, "He who receives you receives Me, and he who receives Me receives Him who sent Me." v. 41 "He who receives a prophet in the name of a prophet shall receive a prophet's reward." The question I have is, "WHAT HAPPENS IF we reject the prophet or reject the righteous man, or refuse to give to one of the little ones a cup of cold water, or refuse to give to our Kingdom brother that asks of us???

And now the rest of verses 41 and 42, " ... and he who receives a righteous man in the name of a righteous man shall receive a righteous man's reward. And whoever in the name of a disciple gives to one of these little ones (or humble folk) even a cup of cold water to drink, truly I say to you he shall not lose his reward."

2. Luke 10:16, "The one who listens to you listens to Me, and the one who rejects you rejects Me; and he who rejects Me rejects the One who sent Me." How about putting this in our promise box, memory pack and fortune cookies? And how about putting our brother or sister who is doing the will of God in the verse? It would (and in truth does) read like this, "The one who listens to [them] listens to Me, and the one who rejects [them] rejects Me; and he who rejects Me..." Or apply this verse to yourself and make it read like this (because it does): "If I reject the

representatives of Jesus, then I am rejecting Jesus Christ Himself, and if I listen to the representatives of Jesus Christ (when they are speaking what Jesus wants), then I am listening to Christ Himself." Or is that too strong? I'll leave the decision to you, and your decision will be put to the test of fire at the Judgement Seat of God. But before you hurry on, go back and read the verse again in your favorite translation! (Remember, our definition of a Kingdom Representative is: anyone that the King has commissioned to represent Him in any regard - but we are not talking about "professional" men of God, or religious men — but those who are totally committed to the will of God and are functioning under His Lordship and His leading!!)

3. The parable of the sheep and the goats: "Then the King will say to those on His right, "Come, you who are blessed of My Father, inherit the Kingdom prepared for you from the foundation of the world" (Matt. 25:34). These got into the Kingdom of God because they gave food, clothing, and shelter to those who are doing the Father's will! "And the King will answer and say to them, Truly, I say to you, to the extent that you did it to one of these brothers of Mine, even the least of them, you did it TO ME!!" (Matt. 25:40)

The reason the others went to hell's "eternal fire" was because they did NOT give food, clothing, and shelter to those who were doing the will of God. "Then He will answer them, saying, 'Truly, I say to you, to the extent that you did not do it to one of the least of these, you did not do it TO ME!!!' And these

90

will go away into eternal punishment, but the righteous into eternal life" (Matt. 12:45-46). Perhaps you may be asking, "To whom does 'the least of these My brothers' refer? Jesus, Himself answered that question in Matthew 12:46-50, "While He was still speaking to the multitudes, behold, His mother and His brothers were standing outside, seeking to speak to Him. And someone said to Him, "Behold, your mother and your brothers are standing outside seeking to speak to You." But he answered the one who was telling Him and said, "Who is My mother and who are My brothers?" And stretching out His hand toward His disciples, He said, "Behold, My mother and My brothers! For WHOEVER SHALL DO THE WILL OF MY FATHER who is in heaven, he IS MY BROTHER AND SISTER AND MOTHER." Also in Luke 8:20,21, "But He (Jesus) answered and said unto them, 'My mother and My brothers are THESE WHO HEAR THE WORD OF GOD AND DO IT' ".

ACCREDITED TO YOUR ACCOUNT

It is interesting to see what things anger certain people. For example, in our presenting the Gospel of the Kingdom to the dear ones, some folks have become angry with us at this point. One dear man said, "Now, just wait a minute here, John, it sounds to me like you are saying that I've got to receive you and your message, and that seems too dogmatic for me!" To which I responded, "I'm perfectly willing not to be an issue here, but let me ask you one question." He said, "o.k." So I said, "Suppose there was a man sent from God whose name was uh, George, and that he was commissioned from God and that he had a message from God, that he is one of the 12 or the 70 that Christ sent out; and that uh, George and Don, as perfect strangers, come to town and that they are not received. What would happen to those dear folks who rejected, uh, George or Don? Won't it be true of them that "it will be more tolerable for the land of Sodom and Gomorrah in the day of judgement, than for that city [or group or person rejecting]??" (Matt. 10:15). My brother agree with me. And whether or not you and I agree on this truth, the game of Life continues any way, and it will all become clear when we stand before the Referee of the Universe!

In our folding brochure on the Kingdom of God, we present the question. "What is Kingdom anarchy or insurrection?" to which is given the following answer, "Kingdom anarchy is: Anyone or anything that fails to cooperate with, or that resists, what the King wants or says, or whom the King sends." Please, dear one, please don't be so defensive at this point that you miss the point. It's so important that we don't!

THE MESSENGER BOY

Suppose a messenger from Western Union or the Post Office comes to your front door with a message for you. But suppose also that the messenger has something about him that you don't like. Do you reject the message because you don't like the messenger? Many servants of God, and representatives of the King are being rejected daily through people's arrogance and ignorance and independence and jealousy and back biting and back stabbing and denominationalistic, ritualistic prejudice that has terrifyingly excluded and limited and restrained and restricted and hindered and persecuted Christ Himself, and it WILL BE accredited to their account as having been done TO CHRIST the way they have treated even the least of those who were doing the will of God!!! IT IS ACCREDITED TO OUR ACCOUNT, (yours and mine) AS HAVING BEEN DONE TO CHRIST THE WAY YOU AND I RELATE TO THE LEAST OF HIS BRETHREN, (THOSE WHO ARE DOING GOD'S WILL).

Remember the Kingdom parable of the vineyard where the King goes on a journey, leaving His vineyard in charge of some hireling share cropper tenants? Later He sent His representatives. Remember how angry the evangelical and liberal church leaders of Christ's day became when Jesus told them this parable? This is another ugly example of Kingdom anarchy. (Matt. 21:33-46 ...Makes interesting reading!)

Lord Jesus Christ, Father God, please grant that we never wrongly relate to the Christ in the least of the brethren, (or sisters) and that we may always correctly relate to the Christ WHEREVER You are found! We repent, O Lord God, for every and any time that we have failed to correctly relate to You. I receive from You, Father, that Godly carefulness, lest I fail to rightly relate to Thee."

AFTERNOON SNACK

Dear one, suppose that Christ becomes the Life of the least of the brothers or sisters that are doing the will of God, and you back-bite, sow discord and suspicion and division against them. Or fail to feed, clothe, or shelter these who are committed to the will of God? May the Precious Judge of all the Universe have mercy on your soul!!! One would not think of biting off his little finger for an afternoon snack — (forgive me for this horrible example) — but think nothing of hurting our spouse, family, loved ones, fellow members of the body of Christ...(forgive you for this horrible sin)!!!

THE HUNTER

I had a dream in which I was the big white game hunter with a big game rifle, going through the tall jungle grass, when, to my horror and dismay, I discovered that our quarry, or prey, was a human being. Sure enough, we killed him, cooked him, and I was just ready to take a big bite out of this hairy arm when I awoke. I was nauseated. I said, "Lord, what are You trying to show me?" And it seemed that the Heavenly Father said, "You people in the body of Christ do WORSE than this when you sow discord among the brethren in your back biting and criticism in the Church of Christ Jesus." Then the Scripture came to mind, "BUT IF YE BITE AND DEVOUR ONE ANOTHER, TAKE HEED [take care] LEST YOU BE CONSUMED BY ONE ANOTHER" (Gal. 5:15 KJ). May all spiritual vampirism and cannibalism cease from within the Church of the Lord Jesus Christ, and from within your life, and mine -once and for all time, immediately!!! In Jesus' Name, AMEN.

KINGDOM ANARCHY

Galatians 5:19-21 gives a list of Kingdom

anarchists who "shall not inherit the Kingdom of God." The list is: "Adultery, fornication, idolatry, witchcraft, hatred, variance (contention), emulations (jealousy), wrath, strife, seditions, heresies, envyings, murders, drunkenness (alcoholism), revellings and such like: of the which I told you in time past, that they which do (practice) such things shall not inherit the Kingdom of God."

Notice that although drunkenness and immorality are sins we recognize as being "bad" and "terrible", yet most Christians don't also see the sins of hatred, variance, wrath, strife, seditions, envyings, and such like to be terrible or bad enough to keep (or kick) people out of the Kingdom of God. I John says that anyone who hates a brother is a MURDERER! One has said that there are more people murdered with the tongue than all the other ways of murder put together.

It is true that practicing alcoholics, fornicators and murderers, (saved or unsaved) will be excluded from the Kingdom of God, (unless these dear ones totally and quickly repent), but backbiters, gossips, character assassinators and those who sow discord among the body of Christ won't make it either! Thus saith the Lord! Some Christians seem to think that there is an invisible asterisk (*) here, directing us to the bottom of the page where in small print we find the words, "except for the 'saved drunks' or the 'saved fornicators' or the 'saved back biters'!

But this is rank heresy and first class stupidity. The Bible says, "...ALL liars (& whore mongers, etc.,) SHALL have their part in the lake which burneth with fire and brimstone: which is the second death!" Rev.21:8. Don't you think this "ALL" includes you if you are a liar or a (whatever else is included in these lists)??? I tell you, dear one, that there has been a false gospel preached in many of our churches that says that "after we have been 'born-again', that we can live and act like hell and we'll go to heaven." But the Gospel of the King and the Kingdom is spelled out VERY clearly in many places like these verses we are quoting and other verses like Matthew 7:21 where Jesus says, "NOT EVERY ONE WHO SAYS TO ME 'LORD', 'LORD', WILL INHERIT THE KINGDOM OF GOD, BUT HE (OR SHE) WHO DOES THE WILL OF MY FATHER WHO IS IN HEAVEN." There are those who sweetly sickly say, "Now dearie, all you got to do is walk the sawdust trail (down the isle) and pray the sinner's prayer 'Godbemercifulto-measinnerandsavemeforchrissakeamen' and then you can go and live like hell and you'll go to heaven ---" Believer, that is damnable baloney! Jesus says, "If you expect to inherit the Kingdom, Brother, you've got to DO My Father's will"!!! (Matthew 7:21). If you have any question about these things, please be respectfully referred to our book, *How To Rule The World or Seek First The Kingdom Of God.*

In I Corinthians 5:11, God indicates that we are not to keep company, or to eat with, a fornicator or alcoholic if he calls himself a brother, but that list also includes "railers" or those critical of others in the body of Christ. Romans 16:17 says that we are to "mark" and "avoid" those "which cause divisions" in the body of Christ. Again, the Lord is concerned for His Bride, hence the quarantine.

But, whether or not we exercise discipline in the body of Christ, nevertheless, IT WILL BE ACCREDITED TO OUR ACCOUNT, AS HAVING BEEN DONE TO CHRIST, THE WAY WE RELATE TO EVEN THE LEAST OF THE CITIZENS OF THE KINGDOM OF GOD -(THOSE WHO ARE DOING THE WILL OF GOD!!!)

Another portion that deals with this same kind of insurrection is I Corinthians 6:8-10, where God says, "You yourselves wrong and defraud, and that your brethren. Or do you not know that the unrighteous shall NOT inherit the Kingdom of God? Do not be deceived; neither fornicators, nor idolaters, nor adulterers, nor effeminate, nor homosexuals, nor thieves, nor the covetous, nor drunkards, nor revilers, nor swindlers, shall inherit the Kingdom of God."

But, thanks be to God, we don't have to be rebels to the King, for the very short next verse says, "And such WERE some of you; but you WERE washed, but you WERE sanctified, but you WERE justified in the Name of the Lord Jesus Christ and in the Spirit of our God" (vs. 11). This means, and the Bible says that these things are forgivable if a person turns away from these things and receives God's deliverance and walks in righteousness.

Christ said that blasphemy of the Holy Spirit is never forgivable, when they said of Him, "That's of the devil"! (Mark 3). Yet how many times have you heard Christians glibly say that about things which may have been of the Holy Spirit?!!! And why does Jesus say that if we call someone an "idiot" or a "fool", we are in danger of hell fire? (Matt. 5:21.22). And remember what He said about causing a little one to stumble? (Matt. 18).

Lord of the Universe, we repent of that hideously destructive assassination, cannibalism and vampirism within the Body of Christ. We see that in order to qualify to be in the Joel's Army of God, that we can't and won't be running one another through. We determine by Your grace before Your face that we shall not be spiritual anarchists or cannibals. For Thy Kingdom's sake. (And for my own soul's sake!) Amen.

CHAPTER 4 — REVIEW

1. Please define "Kingdom Anarchy".
2. Give as many synonyms as you can for Kingdom Anarchy.
3. Give at least 3 (or more) Scriptural examples of Kingdom Anarchy.
4. In the parable of the sheep & goats - what was the difference between them?
5. What was the result in each case?
6. What was the same with both groups?
7. Which one will you be?
8. Who are the "brothers" of Christ and our brothers too—that we do it to—the least of these? (Matt 12:46-50 & Lk.8:20,21)
9. Complete the statement "It is accredited to my account as having been _____ ."
10. What is spiritual vampirism & cannibalism?
11. What is "Blaspheming the Holy Spirit?"
12. Are you going to cannibalize anyone anymore?
13. Do you think a Christian can "live like hell and still go to heaven"?
14. Do you think that you can call Jesus "Lord", and expect to "inherit the Kingdom of God" without "doing the will of the Heavenly Father"? (The answer to this question is found in Matthew 7:21).

CHAPTER 5 — OUTLINE

SUSPICION

I. Gift of Suspicion
II. The True Basis Of Love & A Walk With God
III. Demonstrations Of Demonic Devices
    A. Movie House Of Our Mind or "Hint, Hunch or Humbug"
    B. Thumpity Thump & Flip Flop
    C. Laurel & Hardy or Abbot and Costello
    D. Invisible Wedge Shaped Principalities
    E. Pass The Toast or "Twister Spirits"
    F. It's Curtains For The Enemy
IV. Selected Scriptures On Revelation
VI. Review

5

THE GIFT OF SUSPICION
or
KINGDOM REVELATION

We have a friend named Aleen, who had a friend who was a witch, although Aleen did not know her friend was a witch. This witch would have people pose for a picture instead of signing the guest book. Then the witch would take these pictures and have them dubbed into a compromising photograph so cleverly done that the only way one could tell that it wasn't good ol' brother so and so would be by revelation.

The defeated devil is working increasingly overtime in order to make look good what's bad and to make look bad what's good, so much so that increasingly the only way that we will be able to tell the difference will be by revelation. (Notice: I said revelation, NOT suspicion!)

That's the only way they were able to recognize Jesus and the disciples in those days, and in these days, too. Please allow for the possibility that had you lived during His time that you might not have recognized Him. You might have been one of the religious evangelical leaders of Christ's day, plotting His death. It was the 'fundamentalists' of Christ's day who crucified Him.

They read the Scriptures more, fasted more, led more religious lives, kept the legalistic rules. And we can miss Him today also. Yes you really can!

It's an interesting historical fact, that the thing God brought forth in one generation, has almost always persecuted the thing God does in the next.

The amazing thing about deception is that A DECEIVED PERSON NEVER KNOWS WHEN He IS DECEIVED. Thus, we all need to be very humble, taking heed lest we fall. Do you know all there is to know about God? We don't either. So, could we agree to be very patient with one another as we experience this marvelous adventure of being led into all the truth by God's Holy Spirit?

Jesus spoke in parables not to make the message plain, but to make it obscure or hidden from those not entitled to know. "To you it is granted to KNOW THE MYSTERIES OF the Kingdom of God, but to the rest in parables; in order that seeing they may not see, and hearing they may not understand" Luke 8:10.

And in another place, "At that very time He rejoiced greatly in the Holy Spirit, and said, 'I praise Thee, O Father, Lord of heaven and earth, that Thou didst hide these things from the wise and intelligent and didst reveal them unto babes. Yes, Father, for thus it was well pleasing in Thy sight.' " "All things have been handed over to Me by My Father, and no one

103

knows who the Son is except the Father, and who the Father is except the Son, and anyone to whom the Son wills to reveal Him." "And turning to the disciples, He said privately, 'Blessed are the eyes which see the things you see, for I say to you, that many prophets and kings wished to see the things which you see, and did not see them, and to hear the things which you hear, and did not hear them' " Luke 10:21-24.

Still another example, "And Jesus answered and said to him, 'Blessed are you, Simon Barjonas, because flesh and blood did not reveal this to you, but My Father Who is in heaven.'" Matt. 16:17. This was in response to when "He said to them, 'But who do you say that I am?' And Simon Peter answered and said, 'Thou art the Christ, the Son of the Living God.' " Matt. 16:15,16.

They have perfected the communications media to the extent that they are able to take a number of tapes of a person and from those tapes comprise a thesaurus of words and phrases from which one could manufacture a message, phone conversation, or teaching totally opposite from the original, so that the only way one could tell who's who or what's what would be by a revelation from God.

THE TRUE BASIS OF LOVE
OR A WALK WITH GOD

Contrary to all teaching to the contrary, the true basis of love, or a walk with God is a COMMITMENT OF THE WILL BASED ON THE WILL OF GOD!, not on the basis of thoughts, feelings, imagination, finances, circumstances or intuitions.

DASTARDLY DEMONSTRATIONS OF DEMONIC DEVICES

The following illustrations are hopefully helpful ways we will know, and thus avoid the enemy's attempts to deceive us.

MOVIEHOUSE OF OUR MIND, OR HINT, HUNCH, AND HUMBUG

Sometimes the enemy is able to sneak into the moviehouse of our mind and portray upon the screen of our conscious awareness lying or invalid or deceptive thoughts, imaginations, feelings, suggestions, emotions, intimations, intuitions, perceptions, convictions, conclusions, assumptions, hints, hunches and humbugs that are not the will of God. But, if you've seen the movie before, or have read the story already, and know how the story is supposed to go, you are o.k. So also, the way to always be sure at a time like that is to switch over to the auto-pilot of the Word of God, the Will of God, and the sure leading of the Spirit of God.

ONE MUST NEVER DETERMINE THE WILL OF GOD BY LOOKING AT FEELINGS, FINANCES, OR CIRCUMSTANCES, BUT BY THE WILL OF GOD, THE WORD OF GOD, AND THE VOICE OF GOD!

One area where the enemy is able to be most destructive is the marriage. In our book on marriage,

THE SEXUAL MINISTRY, available by writing to us at K.O.G., P.O. 7123, Minneapolis, MN., 55407, this topic is discussed at length, but here are a few examples.

THUMPITY THUMP AND FLIP FLOP

On Lover's Lane a week before the marriage, while simply holding hands, the heart was going thumpity thump, the stomach was doing flip flop, there was a zzzt behind the eyes, the knees were weak, the bells were ringing, birds were singing, it smelled like spring time, etc. Now, years later, you came home to your pregnant wife and noisy kids, she's got bad breath, hair in disarray, a pimple on her chin, she's got a cold, no make up, and for some reason it doesn't smell like spring time and the birds ain't singing. But you love her! Then when you go to the store for some milk, the gal at the checkout register looks like Delilah, Bathsheba, and Cleopatra all in one body, (a friend of mine just asked me, "What store is this?"), and it smells like spring time, and your heart goes thumpity thump and your stomach does flip flop.

For years, Hollywood and Babylon have pushed this lie that love is based on feelings and flip flops, not on a commitment of the will based on the will of God, and that thumpity thumps and spastic thoughts somehow justify adulterous thoughts and acts.

If the man going through the check out counter has it together and has not accepted the lie, he can say to Delilah, "God bless you, lady," hand her a Kingdom Gospel Contract, and head on home to the loyal wife

of his love. And though, from time to time, the birds don't sing nor bells ring, NEVERTHELESS, THAT LOVE IS SURE AND STRONG AND PURE BECAUSE THAT LOVE IS BASED SOLIDLY IN A FIRM COMMITMENT OF ONE'S OWN WILL, BASED ON THE WILL OF GOD!!! Everything in our walk with God must have the same foundation. Our worship, praise and rejoicing, our reading of the Word, our attendance and tithing, our love for each other, our being led by the Holy Spirit, must all be based on a CHOICE or commitment of our will, based on the Will and Word of God. Thus saith the Lord!

REMEMBER: "We wrestle not against flesh and blood, but against principalities, against powers, against the rulers of the dark-ness of this world, against spiritual wickedness in high places" Eph. 6:12 (KJ).

The following illustrations include several ways in which the defeated enemy tries to bring division and separation and misunderstanding into the body of Christ: The Bible says that "we are not ignorant of his (satan's) devices". II Corinthians 2:11.

LAUREL & HARDY — ABBOT & COSTELLO

Remember in the cartoons or movies where two friends are walking along when a third person from hiding hits one of the two friends? The hit friend, seeing no one but his friend, ASSUMES that this friend hit him, and says to himself, "I can't let my friend hit me for no good reason." So he hauls off and

108

hits his friend, who says, "I can't let my friend hit me for no good reason." So they are fighting while the enemy is full of glee, still in hiding. It's funny in the cartoons, but not so funny in the family or marriage or in church or among friends.

INVISIBLE WEDGE SHAPED PRINCIPALITIES

Imagine that the enemy would sometimes send an invisible wedge shaped principality between you and your friend. If you are not discerning, you may assume that the problem is coming from your friend, and/or your friend from you.

PASS THE TOAST - TWISTER SPIRIT

Imagine a husband and wife sitting at breakfast, when the husband says to her, "Pass the toast." But what he really means is "Darling, I love you so much, I can hardly wait to get home from work to see you, you sweet thing, you are so precious, I'm so glad I married you, and, by the way, would you purty please pass me the toast?" But, remember, all he said was, "Pass the toast." (Maybe he was still waking up.) But suppose she got the wrong impression and that the enemy twisted the intent of his message so that by the time it reached her ears she ASSUMED that he meant, "Hey, you old bag, pass me the toast before I hit you in the mouth." She responds by saying, "WHADDYA MEAN, 'PASS THE TOAST? GIDITCHERSELF!" I've seen this kind of thing happen often in people's interpersonal relationships. But in this illustration, suppose that the husband

THE INVISIBLE WEDGE-SHAPED
PRINCIPALITY

LAUREL & HARDY // ABBOT & COSTELLO

PASS the TOAST OR TWISTER SPIRIT

CURTAINS for the ENEMY

meant something negative, but because of her love and her trust and her faith, she responded sweetly by saying, "Oh darling, I love you too, you precious sweet thing, you, and I can hardly wait to see you, and by the way, here's your toast for my honey." (See our book on THE SEXUAL MINISTRY.) For even though he may have originally meant something negative, he can't help but respond to her faith and trust and love. Get the picture?

One time the husband and wife were arguing, when, suddenly the husband saw "the light" reflected from his wife's wedding ring. He stopped mid-sentence, walked around to where his wife was sitting, gently put his hand in hers, and said, "Darling, I'm on your side!"

HITCHHIKER SPIRIT

We have a friend that people would become aggravated with for no apparent reason. People would want to haul off and hit poor Richard even though he had done nothing to cause this kind of reaction. Finally, a man of God discerned that the enemy had sent an aggravating kind of spirit to follow this person to create this kind of reaction in people. Richard was actually a very friendly guy.

IT'S CURTAINS FOR THE ENEMY

Sometimes this situation exists in circles or in waves or curtains around a person especially called of God or chosen of God for a special work or ministry, and usually to the extent of that ministry's

112

importance in the Kingdom of God. In every case, the LORD HAS GIVEN US POWER OVER THE ENEMY, TO TAKE AUTHORITY OVER THE SITUATION. But in this illustration, when approaching a person, one may feel reactions of rejection, lust, hate, isolation, arrogance, aggravation, confusion, or deception. It is important to KNOW THE PERSON'S HEART because these conditions may only exist in the atmosphere around a person who is called of God and who is, in fact, a loving, accepting, humble, anointed man or woman of God. Sometimes, unless a person is very sharp in discerning, one may interpret as coming from another person something that in reality is not in that person's heart, or being, at all.

Remember: THE ENEMY IS ALWAYS TRYING TO MAKE LOOK BAD WHAT'S GOOD AND TO MAKE LOOK GOOD WHAT'S BAD so that it is always necessary to move in a state of KINGDOM REVELATION or DISCERNMENT. "Evil men do not understand justice, but THOSE WHO SEEK THE LORD UNDERSTAND ALL THINGS" Pr. 28:5. Remember - it's the revelation gifts of knowledge, discernment, wisdom - NOT the gift of suspicion! We've known folks who thought of themselves as being spiritual when in fact they were religiously suspicious and doubting.

A man of God has said that he would rather err in trusting love and be wrong by having trusted with faith and love as a basis 999 times, than to be wrong 1 time in 1000 through unrighteous judging, with suspicion and unbelief as it's wrong basis.

114

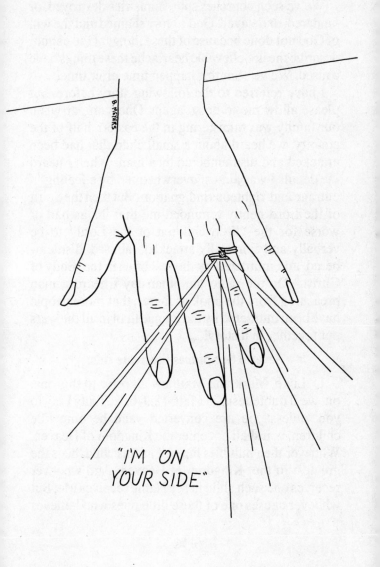

We've seen churches split, ministries destroyed, or hindered, or delayed, God's glory shamed and the will of God not done because of these things. One cannot describe the unbelievable heartache these things have caused. We've seen this happen time after time!

I have referred to the following story before, but please allow me to do so again. One summer when our family was ministering in the eastern half of the country, we heard about a small child that had been attacked and dismembered by a man. When I heard the details I was almost overwhelmed by a feeling of outrage and righteous indignation. But then the Spirit of the Lord gently reminded me that it's as bad or worse for the "little children of the Lord" to be verbally and spiritually attacked, abused, dismembered, and murdered by the rest of us in the Body of Christ. On the radio the other day I heard a man preaching from the book of James, that more people have been murdered by the tongue than in all the wars put together in history!

Several Scriptures illustrate this:

1) Luke, Mark and Matthew all refer to this one, but we'll quote Jesus in Matt. 18:3-6, "...Truly I say to you, unless˙ you are converted and become like children, you shall not enter the Kingdom of Heaven. Whoever then humbles himself as this child, he is the greatest in the Kingdom of Heaven. And whoever receives one such child in My Name receives Me; But whoever causes one of these little ones who believes

116

in Me to stumble, it is better for him that a heavy millstone be hung around his neck, and that he be drowned in the depth of the sea." Here Christ is talking about the humble citizens of the Kingdom.

2) Matt. 5:19-24, "Whosoever therefore shall break one of these least commandments, and shall teach men so, he shall be called the least in the Kingdom of Heaven: but whosoever shall DO and TEACH them, the same shall be called great in the Kingdom of Heaven. For I say unto you, That except your righteousness shall exceed the righteousness of the scribes and Pharisees, ye shall in no case enter into the Kingdom of Heaven.

"Ye have heard that it was said by them of old time, Thou shalt not kill; and whosoever shall kill shall be in danger of the judgement: but I say unto you, That whosoever is angry with his brother shall be in danger of without the judgement: and whosoever shall say to his brother, Raca, (good for nothing) shall be in danger of the council: but whosoever shall say, Thou fool, shall be in danger of hell fire.

"Therefore if thou bring thy gift to the altar, and there rememberest that thy brother hath ought against thee; leave there thy gift before the altar, and go thy way; first be reconciled to thy brother, and then come and offer thy gift." (KJ)

3) I John 3:14-18, "We know that we have passed from death unto life, because we love the brethren. He that loveth not his brother abideth in death. Whosoever hateth his brother is a murderer: and ye know that no murderer hath eternal life abiding in

117

him. Hereby perceive we the love of God, because He laid down His life for us: and we ought to lay down our lives for the brethren. But whoso hath this world's good, and seeth his brother have need, and shutteth up his heart of compassion from him, how dwelleth the love of God in him? My little children, let us not love in word, neither in tongue; but in deed and in truth." (KJ)

I John 4:20-21, "If a man say, I love God, and hateth his brother, he is a liar: for he that loveth not his brother whom he hath seen, how can he love God whom he hath not seen? And this commandment have we from Him, That he who loveth God love his brother also." (KJ)

NAZI SLAUGHTER

It is right to be outraged at the Atlanta Murderer, or the Nazi slaughters, but we need to feel equal or greater outrage at the spiritual, psychic, emotional, or mental murders and assaults and torments WE members of the body of Christ commit against each other as husbands, wives, brothers, sisters, family members, pastors, evangelists, members of the body of Christ - and especially the 'humble ones' who are trying earnestly to fulfill the will of God and the Great Commission - the brothers and sisters and mothers of Christ! When Paul was persecuting the Christians, Jesus said, "Why are you persecuting ME? (Acts 9:4b), and "I am Jesus, Whom you are persecuting"! (vs 5). Notice, Jesus did not say, "I am Jesus, whose people you are persecuting." No, He said to Paul that when he persecuted them, then he persecuted the Christ. And so it is today!

One of the members of our church came to me one day really troubled about a dream he had had. He said, "In this dream, I was stabbing and chopping this person to death. I don't know what this means. Can you tell me?" I said, "No, but let's ask the Lord to be showing you what it means." The next day, he came to me in tears and repenting, said, "God showed me that the man I was murdering - - - was you!" He then confessed that he had been guilty of murmuring, back biting, and sinfully critical of the ministry. Then, through his tears, he asked me to forgive him, which, of course, I did.

THE WISDOM OF GOD

Please study with me for a moment about the nature of this revelation knowledge and wisdom and how it works from this Scripture:

"That your faith should NOT rest on the wisdom of men, but on the power of God. Yet we do speak wisdom among those who are MATURE, a wisdom, however, not of this age, nor of the rulers of this age, who are passing away;

"But we speak God's wisdom in a mystery, the HIDDEN wisdom, which God predestined before the ages to our glory;

"The wisdom which NONE of the rulers of this age has understood; for IF they had understood it, they would NOT have crucified the Lord of glory;

"But just as it is written, 'Things which eye has not seen and ear has not heard, and which have not entered the heart of man, all that God has prepared for those who love Him.'

"For to us God revealed them through the Spirit; for the Spirit searches all things, even the depths of God.

"For who among men knows the thoughts of a man except the spirit of the man which is in him? Even so the thoughts of God no one knows except the Spirit of God.

"Now we have received, not the spirit of the world, but the Spirit who is from God that we might know the things freely given to us by God,

"Which things we also speak, not in words taught by human wisdom, but in those taught by the Spirit, combining spiritual thoughts with spiritual words.

"But a natural man does not accept the things of the Spirit of God; for they are foolishness to him, and he cannot understand them, because they are spiritually appraised.

"BUT HE WHO IS SPIRITUAL (not unspiritual) APPRAISES ALL THINGS, YET HE HIMSELF IS APPRAISED BY NO MAN.

"For who has known the mind of the Lord that he should instruct Him? But we have the mind of Christ" I Cor.2:5-16.

When it says "natural man", most Christians automatically assume that they are not a "natural man" and that this verse does not apply to them. But they are wrong, just as Holy Apostle St Peter was wholly wrong, when Jesus, right after giving Pete the keys, looked at him and said, "Get thee behind Me, satan, for..." Peter, you are thinking like a natural man, or to put it back into the Shakspearian manner of King James: "...thou savourest not the things that be of God, but of man." And if you and I are not careful, we won't "savour" either.

Job's friends were wrong. Eli the priest was wrong with Samuel's mother. David's brothers were wrong when he wanted to kill Goliath. Saul was wrong when he wanted to kill Jonathan. And you may be wrong also! Remember: the greatest key to knowing the will of God is to have a deep Deep DEEP commitment to DO THE WILL OF GOD!!! (John 7:17)

I say again, do you know all there is to know about God? We don't either. But can we agree to be patient with each other in this marvelous adventure of being led into all truth by the Holy Spirit?

MOST DISLIKED BIBLE VERSE

I have a least favorite Scripture. I don't like it, but I must agree with it.(Truth doesn't change just because I don't like it, or because I don't agree with it. But I agree with all Scripture, because it is God's love letter to me). Remember that Verse where Jesus, after walking with the disciples for three years, told them, "I have many more things to say to you, but you cannot bear them now." John 16:12? I don't want the Lord to have to say that to me. Remember that definition of the word RUT = "a shallow grave with the end knocked out" ? God, deliver us from our ruts,

121

and from every negative conditioning of our thinking, every limitation on our expectancy, every barrier to overflowing faith!!! And cause us to be a people that You can lead into all truth, revealing that which is to come, revealing to us the things of Christ. In Jesus' Name, Amen.

This, then, is the means by which we recognize the citizens and messages and representatives of the Kingdom of God. A representative of the Kingdom of God is ANYONE THE KING HAS CHOSEN TO REPRESENT HIM IN ANY REGARD AND WHO IS FUNCTIONING WITH THE INTEGRITY OF THE KING.

"I praise Thee, O Father, Lord of heaven and earth, that Thou didst hide these things from the wise and intelligent, and didst reveal them to babes." Luke 10:21.

In the last two chapters, we have been talking about the importance of unity in the Body of Christ, and now, about knowing the will of God. Here is something that ties these two thoughts together:

BODY GUIDANCE

Please allow me to refer to these following points again, also. There should be more allowance in the Body of Christ for each other to be led sovereignly by God, led by the Holy Spirit. Romans 8:14 "For as many as are led by the Spirit of God, they are the Sons of God" (KJ). Sometimes God leads in strange ways and it behooves us not to be critical of the way God may be sovereignly leading. Acts 21:14 gives an example of a difference of opinion, that was only solved by the dear ones in lovingly committing this brother to the grace of God and saying, "The will of the Lord be done!" Instead, sometimes we will purposely, psychically intimidate and alienate our brother or sister when we think they are not doing the will of God as we see it for them. But this is not fair or wise. We can tell them what we think, but then it is our responsibility not to judge or be critical. Their God, Jesus Christ, has a right to lead them, without obtaining your approval. In that case, we lovingly commend them to the grace of God and love them and pray for them and keep the door open to them. If they are wrong, they will have difficulty enough, now and later, without us adding to their problem our judgement and criticism. Jesus is still saying to us today, "What is that to thee? Follow thou Me!" (John 21:22b)

Recently, I became freshly impressed that is is not enough for me to accept Christ as my Lord alone, but it is also necessary for me to accept and receive Christ Jesus as The Lord of my brother and sister in Christ...as your Lord too!!

God be merciful to all of us as we seek diligently to please Him in everything.

Romans 14 is good in this regard. Now we are NOT talking about things in the Bible that God has clearly said is sin. But there are a multitude of other areas where we are guilty of judging. Verse 4, "Who art thou that judgest another man's servant? To his own master he standeth or falleth. And God is able to make him stand." (KJ)

So, we see that there is such a deep need for us to love each other unconditionally, without criticism, strings or walls, character assassination or resentment. The Lord says that it is not enough to love one another tolerantly, but that we are to "obey the truth through the Spirit unto unfeigned love of the brethren, see that ye LOVE ONE ANOTHER WITH A PURE HEART FERVENTLY!!!" (I Pet. 1:22).

We worship You, Oh Lord God of the Universe, Lord Jesus Christ and we also will be careful to honor You, and appreciate You, in our brother and in our sister! We repent for not having rightly related to You in the least of the brothers and sisters. And ask that by Your grace we will always rightly relate to You wherever You are found.

We ask You Lord Jesus for the Spirit of Wisdom, Revelation and the Knowledge of our God to rest upon us, unceasingly - increasingly. Yea Lord, Be our Life. Love through us with a pure and fervent practical "I Corinthians 13" and "I John" type of love. Please help us always to be rightly related to You in the dear ones, and to never be wrongly related to You, in them. Oh Dear Father, always BE our LIFE, and help us to always relate to our fellow Christians as though You are their life, too. In Jesus Christ's Name we pray and believe.

Amen.

CHAPTER 5 — REVIEW

1. Complete this sentence - The defeated devil is working over-time trying to make look good and _____ to make look bad _____ .
2. How will we know the difference?
3. What religious group responsible for crucifying Christ would compare with today?
4. What is the only way the disciples were able to recognize Christ? Then — now?
5. T or F - That which God did yesterday has almost always persecuted what God is doing today.
6. Yes or no - Do you know all there is to know about God?
7. T or F - A deceived person never knows when they are deceived?
8. T or F - Jesus spoke in parables to make the message plain.
9. Complete the sentence - The true basis of love or a walk with God is _____ .
10. Name at least 5 things that are totally unreliable indications of the will of God.
11. Name at least 2 things that are always reliable indications of the will of God.
12. Complete this Kingdom principle: "One must never determine the will of God by looking at a)_____ b)_____ c)_____ but by looking at d)_____ e)_____ & f)_____ .
13. Name at least 5 symptoms of "being in love" that are not at all valid in determining whether or not

125

one is loving according to the Will and Word of God.

14. If a person "falls out of love" with one's spouse and "falls in love" with someone else - does this justify adulterous thoughts and/or actions?

15. Explain as briefly as possible the following illustrations on disunity and deception:
    a) Laurel & Hardy
    b) Invisible Wedge Shaped Principalities
    c) Pass the Toast
    d) Hitch hiker
    e) Curtains for the enemy.

16. What sins in the body of Christ are equal to or worse than a child murderer or the nazi-criminals?

17. On the basis of John 7:17, what is the best way to know the will of God?

18. What was the definition given of a "rut"?

19. Define "Kingdom Representative".

20. In addition to receiving Christ as OUR Lord, what is also necessary in our attitude toward our brother/sister in Christ?

21. What is meant by the phrase "psychic intimidation"?

22. What does Rom.14:4 say?

23. How does I Peter 1:22 say we are to love each other?, (See also 4:8).

Chapter 6 - Outline
IMPALED

I. Getting Back What We Give To Others.

II. "Touching The Lord's Anointed".

III. Declaration of Holy War.

IV. "Hit List".

V. Paul's "Hit List".

VI. Review

6

IMPALED ON A YARDSTICK

"Now, where in the world would you get a chapter title like this?" you may be asking. "Why, from the Bible!" would be my reply.

"Judge not, that ye be not judged." "For with what judgement ye judge, ye shall be judged: and with what MEASURE ye mete, it shall be MEASURED to you again." "And why beholdest thou the mote that is in thy brother's eye, but considerest not the beam that is in thine own eye?" "Or how wilt thou say to thy brother, Let me pull out the mote out of thine eye; and, behold, a beam is in thine own eye?" "Thou hypocrite, first cast out the beam of thine own eye; and then shalt thou see clearly to cast out the mote out of thy brother's eye." "Therefore all things whatsoever ye would that men should do to you, do ye even so to them: for this is the law and the prophets." Words of Jesus from Matthew 7.

When our Lord tells us not to judge, He is not asking us to be either naive, spastically undiscerning

128

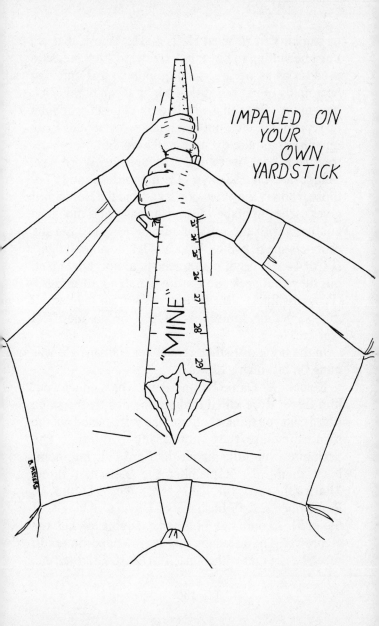

or stupid. Part of what He is saying here is that we must be willing to have the same yard stick measure used on us as we are using on others. It is amazing how many of us can "dish it out" but can't "take it"; how many of us can give advice or counsel or rebuke or reprimand, etc., but are unable, (or should I say unwilling) to take even a small amount of the same treatment back in return! Though the Word says "Judge not!", it also says, "Try the spirits..." and "Try those who say they are apostles..." and the Holy Spirit gives us the gift of the "discerning of spirits" (not to be confused with the gift of suspicion), and "Let the prophets speak two or three, and let the other judge." (I Cor.14:29) "Evil men understand not judgement: but they that seek the Lord understand all things." (Proverbs 28:5) "But he that is spiritual judgeth all things, yet he himself is judged of no man." (I Cor.2:15).

In the book of Esther, remember Haman? He was hung on his own gallows.

Remember Daniel's lion's den? The men who put him there were killed in the same den by the same lions! Can you think of others who were meted out the same measure they meted out to others? The Scripture even talks about the Lord "paying them back double"! Remember the men that threw Shadrach into the fiery furnace? (Dan.3:2). Remember Nabal, husband of David's Abigail? (I Sam.25). Remember Pharaoh pledging to kill the Hebrews? The measure that he intended others to meet, he got met with, himself!!! (Ex.10:28). Etc., etc.

130

Paul says, "Who art thou, that judgest another man's servant? Before his own Master he standeth or falleth. And God is able to make him stand!" Remember, it is not enough for us to accept Jesus as our Lord only, but IT IS also NECESSARY FOR US TO RECEIVE JESUS CHRIST AS LORD OF OUR BROTHER (and sister).

Are you one of those who likes to wrongly quote the Scripture: "There is One Mediator between God and man: the Man Christ Jesus, AND ME!!!" (The "and me" should not, MUST not, be added.)

AN UNFORGIVEABLE SIN
or
BLASPHEMING THE HOLY SPIRIT

Blaspheming the Holy Spirit = saying something is of the devil that is of God's Holy Spirit. I have heard dear Christians say, "Oh, he (or it) is of the devil," when in fact, the person or the thing was of God!!! Jesus says that this sin will NEVER BE FORGIVEN! — yet Christians do this too often. Matthew 12:31.

(If you think that you have committed the "unforgivable sin" please see our treatment of this in our book, *How To Rule The World or Seek First The Kingdom Of God.*)

"If you offend or cause one of these little ones (the disciples, or those who are doing the will of God), to stumble or to fall, better that you never were born, or that you had a millstone hung around your neck and that you be dropped into the deepest part of the sea."

131

(Words from our Sweet Gentle Saviour, in Matthew 18:6; Mark 9:42; Luke 17:2; and Matthew 5:22.)

Let's take a look at this Matthew 5:22 in the Amplified Bible: God is speaking, "But I say to you that EVERY ONE who continues to be angry with his brother or harbors malice [enmity of heart] against him shall be liable to and unable to escape the punishment imposed by the court; and WHOEVER speaks contemptuously and insultingly to his brother shall be liable to and UNABLE TO ESCAPE THE PUNISHMENT imposed by the Sanhedrin, and WHOEVER says, 'You cursed fool!' - 'You empty-headed idiot!' shall be liable to and unable to escape the hell (Gehenna) of fire." God says, "Whoever" and "To his brother". "Whoever" includes Christians and "brother" includes your brother (and your sister) (and your spouse) in the Lord!!! It is a deceived person who says that Christians cannot go to hell, when God Himself says otherwise in places like Hebrews 6:4-6 & 10:23-31 & Mat.24:13, etc. This kind of "eternal security" breeds infernal insecurity!

Again, Jesus Himself says, "If you call your brother a fool, a liar, an empty headed idiot, or stupid, you are in danger of the judgement of hell fire." (Words from our Gentle Jesus.) Matthew 5. Hmmm, I wonder why He said that??? Do we really believe it?? I wonder if the same danger is present when we have that attitude toward our friend in our thinking? What does the Lord say, "If we hate our brother, (or sister), we are a murderer!" I John 4:15. (That's what He says!)

132

TOUCHING THE LORD'S ANOINTED"

There is that in the Christian vernacular what is known as "touching the Lord's anointed". In order to adequately define the term as it is (or should be), used, we will refer to the Scriptures from which the phrase comes: I Chronicles 16:21,22 says, "He, (God), suffered no man to do them wrong: yea, He reproved kings for their sakes, saying, 'TOUCH NOT MINE ANOINTED, AND DO MY PROPHETS NO HARM.' "!!!

O.K., we have the Lord's command, now let's look at the Lord's application of that command. It really makes for interesting reading, (doesn't it all!!!), I Samuel 24:6, "And he said unto his men, 'The Lord forbid that I should do this thing unto...the Lord's anointed, to stretch forth mine hand against him, seeing he is the anointed of the Lord' ".

But LOOK at the situation here where this principle is being applied! David is already the rightful king!!! He has already been anointed and prophesied over! The "Anointed" man about whom he is speaking and "the Anointed" to whom this principle applies is: 1) Demon possessed! (18:10), 2) A murderer! (22:17), 3) Has lied, 4) Has stolen David's wife! (25:44), 5) Has tried to kill David repeatedly! (19:1), 6) Tried to kill his own son! (20:33), 7) Becomes a consulter of a witch, (28:7) for a seance, etc., etc., etc... This, THIS IS THE LORD'S ANOINTED ???? But the exact same temptation comes again two chapters later in 26:9b, & 11a,

133

"Destroy him not: for WHO CAN STRETCH FORTH HIS HAND AGAINST THE LORD'S ANOINTED, AND BE GUILTLESS?" "The Lord forbid that I should stretch forth mine hand against the Lord's anointed."! Why just think of it! Saul's kingdom had ALREADY been taken away from him, and his right to be king - his right to live, was gone. Plus, as we said, he was stark raving demon possessed! You mean to tell me that HE'S NOT TO BE TOUCHED ???

WAR DECLARED

But note one further fact: when David does discover that someone else did touch the Lord's anointed, he not only went into mourning along with his friends, but he executed the people who did touch this "Lord's anointed". But what about you? What about us??? Have you been critical of spiritual leaders? Have you gossiped about them? Have you been wrongly judgemental? O.K., maybe they didn't do it YOUR way, or follow what YOU thought they should do, or say it the way YOU thought they should, or, or, or, or... But let me ask you, were they devil possessed? Did they murder anybody? O.K., maybe they did steal somebody's wife (or divorce their own), maybe they did beg for money when they should have done it the "Mueller Method", (though the beggar went to heaven !) Or, maybe they were too exclusivistic, or arrogant, or preached the "Grand Snatch Rupture Doctrine", or maybe they didn't!!!

But tell me dear one, did they actually murder any one? Were they devil possessed??? Were they worse than Saul??? If they were not, and we "touched" them, mark my words, if we criticized them behind their back and did "roast preacher" on them and "bit" them psychically or devoured them spiritually, then THUS SAITH THE LORD, IT HAS BEEN ACCREDITED TO OUR ACCOUNT, AS HAVING BEEN DONE TO CHRIST, THE WAY WE HAVE RELATED TO EVEN THE LEAST OF THOSE WHO ARE DOING THE WILL OF GOD!!!!!!!

In Galatians 5, Paul gives some insight, "...by love serve one another." "For all the law is fulfilled in one word, even in this; Thou shalt love thy neighbor as thyself." "But if ye bite and devour one another, take heed that ye be not consumed one of another."! "Now the works of the flesh are...hatred, variance, emulations, wrath, strife, seditions, ...envyings,...and such like...that they which do such things shall NOT inherit the Kingdom of God"!!! Then, in conclusion, Paul gives us perhaps the greatest reason why we criticize..."Let us not be desirous of vain glory, provoking one another, ENVYing one another."! James puts it this way, "But if ye have bitter ENVYING and strife in your hearts, glory not, and lie not against the truth." "This wisdom descendeth not from above, but is earthly, sensual, devil-ISH." "For where envying and strife is, there is confusion and every evil work." "But the wisdom that is from above is first pure, then peaceable, gentle, and easy to be

135

entreated, full of mercy and good fruits, without partiality, and without hypocrisy." "And the fruit of righteousness is sown in peace of them that make peace." Once again, I remind you of the last verse in the Old Testament which says that if we don't start loving each other, God will "smite the earth with a curse."!!!!!!!!!!!!!!!!

"HIT LIST"

Who is on your personal psychic "Hit List"? You don't like Tammi's make up? (don't you wish you were as purty?)

Have you been critical of Oral's hospital, (I hope you never need it!) or Jimmy's swagger? (God grant that you become at least as great, and at least as humble,) or Moral's majority, or Billy's success, or Kenneth's faith, or Pat's program or Robert's glass church? Add your own name's and your own pet peeves at your own risk? God is listening and watching, and promises to measure you by your own yardstick, and "mete your own measure"...on you!!!

PAUL'S HIT LIST

Look at Paul's yardstick and Paul's hit list in Philippians 1, "...many of the brethren..." and "Some indeed preach Christ even of envy and strife...", (no make-up mentioned yet, but wait, the list continues), "The one preach Christ of contention, not sincerely, supposing to add affliction to my bonds." Now look at Paul's scathingly vituperative conclusion: "What then? notwithstanding, EVERY WAY, whether in

136

pretense, or in truth, CHRIST IS PREACHED; AND THEREIN DO I REJOICE, YEA, AND WILL REJOICE"!!!!!!! In other words, there may be men of God that have had wrong motives in their ministry, but Jesus is being preached, and in spite of the imperfections or abuses, Christ is being preached and folks are coming to God. Instead of criticizing, Paul rejoices that Jesus is being preached!

I am recommending that this be your reaction also. Which brings us to the next subject called, "The Rule of A Right Spirit".

Before we do though, I want to just mention one other point. David not only refused to touch the Lord's anointed, but he executed those who did. Let me ask you: WHAT DID YOU DO THE LAST TIME SOME ONE MURDERED, MOLESTED, MAIMED, MARRED, MUGGED OR OTHERWISE MESSED WITH THE "LORD'S ANOINTED" IN YOUR PRESENCE???

Here, I think of Franky Schaeffer's book, *ANGER: The Myth of Neutrality.* What would you do if you were sitting at a restaurant in polite company, and some loudmouth, devil possessed drunk, came over and started abusing a lady in your group??? I dare say, would most of you be a silly, weak kneed, sissy??? Would you allow the dastardly and diabolical dismembering of your sweet sister??? Did you think that the Bible says, "When someone slaps your sister, that YOU should turn the other cheek?"

According to our law in this country, if you are "along for the ride" and some crime is committed by your party, then you are equally guilty by association. I talk about this in another place, but I personally invite you to declare a "Holy War", and determine that never again, will you allow the psychic dismembering of a brother or sister to take place in your presence. My decision to do this has led to some confrontation. I have had to plead with, and sometimes rebuke certain family members or close friends or people that I really wanted to impress, but I had a clear choice of offending them OR, of offending the Holy Ghost. Believe me, a true disciple of Jesus has already made up his mind who to offend. Anyone who will compromise, wilt or sell out under this kind of pressure is a spiritual prostitute. We have defined spiritual prostitution as that which "sells out, or compromises, in order to obtain, gain, retain or maintain the favor of man instead of God." Spiritual prostitution is the worst kind of all! A physical prostitute knows what she is, and so do others, but a spiritual prostitute pretends that he, or she, is spiritual.

Father God, I repent for my cannibalizing of others. Help me never to murder others with my mouth — or allow others to in my presence. Help me always to rightly relate to you — in the least of these. Amen

CHAPTER 6 — REVIEW

1. From what Scripture comes the thought of being impaled on a yardstick?
2. Give at least two Scriptural examples of people who were impaled on their own yardstick, so to speak.
3. Complete this thought: "It is not only necessary for us to receive Jesus Christ as our Lord but also the Lord of _____.
4. Define "Blaspheming the Holy Spirit".
5. What is deserved by those who "cause one of these little ones to stumble or fall"?
6. Who are "these little ones"?
7. What are we in danger of if we call our brother "stupid"?
8. What (briefly) is meant by "touching the Lord's anointed"?
9. Name several negative things about the "anointed" one about whom David was referring, that he refused to "touch".
10. Complete this Kingdom Principle: "It is accredited to our account, as having been done to Christ _____.
11. All the law is fulfilled in what word? _____
12. Name at least 5 things related to this study that will keep folks from inheriting God's Kingdom.
13. What is perhaps the greatest single reason for cannibalism?
14. Is it possible to always keep a "right spirit"?

Chapter 7 - Outline

THE RULE OF A RIGHT SPIRIT

I. My Daughter's Heresy.

II. The King's Greatest Secret.

III. Sweet Revenge.

IV. Pity - Not Envy.

V. Hidden Curse In The Lord's Prayer.

VI. How To Handle Gossip About Yourself.

VII. Another Secret.

VIII. Conclcusion

IX. Review

7

THE RULE OF A RIGHT SPIRIT

SCRIPTURES

"Let the righteous smite me; it shall be a kindness: and let him reprove me; it shall be an excellent oil, which shall not break my head." Psalm 141:5a,b.

"It is necessary that the offense comes, but woe to him by whom the offense comes" Words of Jesus. Matthew 18:7

"Count it all joy..." Sermon on the mount. Matt. 5

"Until 70 times 7." Matthew 18:22

Bitterness = "Take care, lest any root of bitterness springing up, defile many." Eph.4:31 & Hebrews 12:15.

Always forgive everyone for everything. Matt. 6.

"If we walk in the light as He is in the light..." I John 1:7.

"Forgive us our debts, even as we forgive our debtors." The Lord's Prayer. Matthew 6

"For if you will not forgive your brother his trespass against you, neither will your heavenly Father forgive you your trespasses." (First verse following the Lord's Prayer.) Matt.6:15. (jb)

"I will avenge their disobedience, when your obedience is made full." New Testament. II Corinthians 10:6.

"LET THE RIGHTEOUS SMITE ME"

or

THE RULE OF A RIGHT SPIRIT

The Scriptures are very clear about the fact that we are always responsible before God to obtain and maintain a right spirit, or heart attitude. This is a Kingdom Rule that applies first, last and always. For if we have a wrong spirit or heart attitude - then we're wrong Wrong WRONG, no matter how right we are! First let us establish the fact that it is both necessary, and possible to obtain and maintain a right spirit and heart attitude! (See our presentation of "The King's Greatest Secret!")

Someone has said that "it is better to be wrong with a right spirit than to be right with a wrong spirit". And, of course, it is better still to be right with a right spirit! But the beautiful thing is, that when our hearts are right, then the Holy Spirit can lead us into all the truth.

MY DAUGHTER'S HERESY!

One day, one of my darling daughters very innocently said some rank heresy. She said, "Nobody's Perfect!" I replied very sweetly, "Who told you that lie?" Then I gently went on to share the command of Christ in Matthew 5, "Be ye therefore perfect, EVEN AS your Father which is in heaven is

142

perfect.'"! I then went on to explain to her how God has made it possible for us.

It is not only possible, but NECESSARY for us to keep a right spirit. If it is not possible, then we need to change all those Scriptures about "All things are possible to him that believeth"! (Mark 9:23) and "I can do all things through Christ"!!! to read "some things" or "many things" or "most things" or "a few things"!!! To quote an old friend, "I refuse to let my (or my daughter's) faith, no matter how little, be limited by your unbelief, no matter how great!!!"

The same thing applies to the saying, "I'm only human" or "They're only human." Bible says that those of us who are in Christ are SUPER HUMAN!!! In II Peter 1:4, God says that we are "Become partakers of The Divine Nature." and again in I Peter 2:9 God says, "But ye are a chosen generation, a royal priesthood, an holy nation, a peculiar people; that ye should show forth the praises of Him who hath called you out of darkness into His marvelous light."!!!

One of the biggest lies the enemy has ever told us, and that we have too often come to believe as truth, is the lie that we cannot keep a right spirit consistently! God says we can (and must) keep a right spirit! So we need to decide who we are going to believe! In I Corinthians 10:13, the Lord says, "There hath no temptation taken you but such as is common to man: but God is faithful, who will not let you to be tempted above what you are able; but will with the temptation also make a way to escape, that ye may be able to bear it."

Suppose I were to ask you if you are an idolater or an idol worshipper. I'm sure that you have no little idols that you bow down to and worship, yet THE WORST IDOLATRY OF ALL IS THAT IDOLATRY THAT EXALTS A PROBLEM TO A PLACE GREATER THAN GOD'S ABILITY TO SOLVE!!!

If it were not possible to keep a right spirit, then to that extent, we could blame God Himself for our wrong spirit. In fact, THE REVELATION OF THE POSSIBILITY AND THE NECESSITY OF CONSISTENT RIGHTEOUSNESS, PROVIDES THE TRUE BASIS OF REPENTANCE!!! In other words, IT IS IMPOSSIBLE FOR GOD TO FORGIVE WHAT I AM MAKING AN EXCUSE FOR!!! That is to say, as long as I am excusing, I am not repenting. A lady spent about 45 minutes one time telling me about only some of her husband's faults. I said to her, "Dear one, I believe the total solution to the problem would be for you to assume 100% of the responsibility." I had not yet mentioned the fact that he was to take the same medicine! For you see, a relationship must not be fifty-fifty but one hundred-one hundred. Remember how the prophets often did "Vicarious repentance", that is, they would identify themselves with the sin of the people for whom they were interceding, as though it were their own. So must we.

THE KING'S GREATEST SECRET!

Here, we refer you to the secrets we shared earlier about the life and death importance of knowing Knowing KNOWING the revelation about Christ

144

actually Being our Life!!! Like a course in school, we haven't graduated from spiritual kindergarten until we KNOW this secret in a practical way. We will go on from this point assuming you know that Secret. If you don't, please go back and get the reality of it within your heart and guts before you continue!!! For this is necessary to the obtaining and maintaining a right spirit.

SWEET REVENGE

"VENGEANCE IS MINE, I WILL REPAY," saith the Lord."! (Ro.12:19).

Here, we would like to tell you how to "get back at" your enemy! The Bible and the Lord Jesus tells us how to get sweet revenge! And while some may think we are doing "heresy" at this point, we are asking that you be patient with us for just a minute for perspective. Thanks.

"Kill 'em with kindness" and "slay them with love," as the sayings go. The Scripture puts it this way, "Therefore if thine enemy hunger, feed him; if he thirst, give him drink: for in so doing thou shalt heap coals of fire on his head." Romans 12:20. We have counselled with many people who have been crippled with bitterness and resentment that we have been able to help; and this is part of the counsel that we give. We don't tell them to not wish for vengeance. We simply tell them that if they want revenge, that God is the Great Avenger who is in the business of "paying back", of vengeance, of settling accounts! And since this is the case, we encourage the dear ones to simply turn it all over to Him, give it to Him, let the Great Avenger, the Lord Jesus Christ do it !!!

But before we leave this subject of revenge, please consider the above quoted Scripture in context: "Be kindly affectioned one to another with brotherly love; in honor preferring one another."

"Bless them which curse you: bless, and curse not." "Recompense to no man evil for evil..." "If it be possible, as much as lieth in you, live peaceably with all men." "Dearly beloved, avenge not yourselves, but rather give place unto wrath: for it is written, 'Vengeance is Mine; I will repay', saith the Lord." "Be not overcome of evil, but overcome evil with good." Romans 12: verses 10,14,17a,18,19 & 21.

PITY, NOT ENVY

Actually, your enemy, (or your friend), who is persecuting the Christ in someone else is more to be pitied than to be resented. (Note the teaching about the yardstick). Would you like to fall into the hands of the God of Vengeance? Not me! Therefore, with godly fear and trembling, we work out our salvation, knowing that: IT SHALL BE ACCREDITED TO OUR ACCOUNT, AS HAVING BEEN DONE TO CHRIST, THE WAY WE HAVE RELATED TO EVEN THE LEAST OF THOSE WHO ARE DOING THE WILL OF GOD!!! (Matthew 25.)

For, if Christ is your Life, and is Lord within your life, and you are doing God's will for your life, then when they persecute you, they are, in fact, persecuting the Christ!

HIDDEN CURSE IN THE LORD'S PRAYER???

"And forgive us our debts, as we forgive our debtors." (a direct quotation from the Lord's Prayer! And here are the very next verses immediately following the Lord's Prayer: "For IF ye forgive men their trespasses, your Heavenly Father will also forgive you:" "But if ye forgive not men their trespasses, neither will your Father forgive your trespasses." (Matt.6:15) In other words, every time we pray the Lord's Prayer, we are in fact praying, "Lord, I want You to be just exactly as forgiving toward me as I am toward everyone else."!!! You are praying "Lord, if I'm unforgiving toward anyone, I don't want You to forgive me either!" "Then said He unto His disciples, 'It is impossible but that offences will come: but woe unto him, through whom they come!" "It were better for him that a millstone were hanged about his neck, and he cast into the sea, than that he should offend one of these little ones." Luke 17. Then Matthew picks up the story in Matthew 18: "Then came Peter to Him, (Jesus) and said, 'Lord, how oft shall my brother sin against me, (in one day -Lk.17), and I forgive him? Till seven times?' " "Jesus saith unto him, 'I say not unto thee, "Until seven times": but, "Until seventy times seven." ' "

This thought is reflected again in Matthew 18:23-35 where the story is told of a master who had two slaves, the first of which owed him a very great amount of money. He pleaded with the master not to send him to jail for non payment and was in fact tentatively excused for the whole amount. He then

147

immediately proceeded to send his fellow slave to prison for his non-payment of just a few pennies. When his master found out about this injustice, he reinstated the former indebtedness, and said to him, "Shouldest not thou also have had compassion on thy fellow servant, even as I had pity on thee? And his lord was wroth (teed off), and delivered him to the tormentors, till he should pay all that was due unto him. So likewise SHALL MY HEAVENLY FATHER DO ALSO UNTO YOU, IF YE FROM YOUR HEARTS FORGIVE NOT EVERY ONE HIS BROTHER THEIR TRESPASSES."! A good Kingdom Principle to follow is: "ALWAYS FORGIVE EVERYONE FOR EVERYTHING!!!"

HOW TO HANDLE GOSSIP ABOUT YOURSELF

Joey and I were at a television studio one day where we got a chance to talk with Louis L'Amour. On that same show, a question was discussed as to what we should do if we happen to walk into a room where we can't help overhearing untrue gossip about ourselves. One answer given by someone was that we should slink away in shame and humiliation. (My friend just heard this, and said, "No cotton pickin' way!") Another thought was that one should go on in pretending nothing happened. The official answer of etiquette given was that one should walk up to the situation, announce that you had overheard the conversation, and that you felt that it was rude, crude and untrue of the people to have acted as they did, then simply to turn and quickly leave, leaving the gossipers with the problem. What would you do?

Our suggestion would be for you to (of course) be led by the Holy Spirit in this and every situation, but there are additional guidelines given in Scripture for times like this. Our counsel is that you first of all, pray, to make sure you are in the Spirit, right with God, ask for wisdom, (Jas.1:5) then praise the Lord and rejoice in Him. (Phil.4:4) Then go to the people and ask them if what you heard was correct. It may not have been, you know, as they could have been practicing a play, or otherwise using a name applying to someone else, or were repeating what someone else may have said or some other misunderstanding. So, the first thing in the conversation is to get the facts straight. If they were gossiping about you, ask them gently to repent and forgive them if they do, every day 70 x 7. If they don't repent, bless them in the Name of the Lord, perhaps think of something good to do for them, forgive them from your heart, and prepare to weep for them and pray for them when God Himself begins to take vengeance upon them for their cannibalism.

Next, if the person is a Christian, we recommend that you find a neutral third party, and some one they will respect, and go with that other party to the person who offended you, and appeal to them. Then, if they don't listen to reason, take the matter to the group of church people to which they belong. If they won't listen to reason then, practice spiritual quarantine, turn the person over to Yahweh God and let The Almighty deal with them.

Sometimes the way to obtain and/or maintain/retain a right spirit is to follow God's formula for rightly relating. For example, God says in I John 1:7, "But if we walk in the light, as He is in the light, we have fellowship one with another, and the blood of Jesus Christ His Son cleanseth us from all (not most, but all) sin." But notice how so many of us so much of the time get this one turned around backwards. We say, "Well, FIRST I'll get a right spirit, then PERHAPS I'll have fellowship, then MAYBE finally I'll walk in the light with my brother (or sister), and talk with him about the offense, but probably not." Sometimes the way to get (or keep) a right spirit is to go to our brother and "walk in the light" and get it out into the open where it can be looked at for what it really is! Most of the time this act alone will clear everything up. Like an old friend once said, "Communication dispels deception." Many times it does.

ANOTHER SECRET

Please keep this perspective in mind. The eyes of The Lord are looking for those who will qualify to sit on His throne with Him. But He will not prostitute His Glory and unlimited Power and wealth on the unqualified. So, He is in the process of qualifying us. Here is a theory that I have. I believe that in the ages to come, the "Overcomers" will travel from place to place in space with the speed of thought, ruling over galaxies of gold!!! And that, as Arthur E. Bloomfield says, "The earth will serve as a seed planet to populate the Universe!" Moses was disqualified from entering into the Promised Land because he got a wrong spirit, and so will we be disqualified, if we don't learn to keep our's right.

Father God, once again I repent for every time I have sinned against my brother or sister in Christ — when I murdered or maimed them with my mouth. And I forgive everyone for everything. I repent for every time I have had a wrong attitude. I know that You can live Your Life through me. Please, now and always — be my Righteousness. Love others through me. Help me always rightly relate to others. In Jesus Name. Amen.

CONCLUSION

In brief, although this principle is shared in detail in the presentation of the King's Greatest Secret, the way to be perfect is to reckon, or consider, our self to have been crucified, dead, buried, resurrected, ascended, glorified and reigning with CHRIST NOW LIVING IN US AS OUR LIFE!!!

CHAPTER 7 — REVEIW

1. Is it possible to always keep a right spirit?
2. Which is better, to be wrong with a right spirit or to be right with a wrong spirit?
3. What is better still?
4. Complete the statement: "I refuse to let my faith, no matter how small, be limited by _____ .
5. What is perhaps the worst idolatry of all?
6. In this lesson, what provides perhaps the best basis of repentance?
7. In this chapter, what is one thing that it is impossible for God to forgive?
8. In our relating to others in the body of Christ, what is better than a 50-50 relationship?
9. What is meant by "vicarious repentance"?
10. Briefly, what is "The King's Greatest Secret"?
11. What is the best way of getting revenge?
12. What is "the hidden curse" in the Lord's Prayer?
13. At least how many times must we be willing to forgive our brother or sister each and every day?
14. Complete the thought, "Communication dispels.
15. What does it mean to "walk in the light" with our brother?
16. Why was Moses disqualified from entering the Promised Land?
17. Complete the theory thought, "The 'Overcomers' will travel from place to place _____ ."

CHAPTER 8 — Outline
HEADSHIP

I. The Theocracy.

II. What, When and Where Is The Kingdom Of God.

III. Selected Verses On The Kingdom Of God.

IV. The Mighty Right Now God!

V. How To Join The Kingdom Of God.

VI. What Is A Citizen Of The Kingdom Of God.

VII. "Headship" and Intimidation.

VIII. Review

8

HEADSHIP, DISCIPLESHIP, DIVINE ORDER & SUBMISSION
or
THE THEOCRACY

Wow! What a subject to talk about! But we feel that it ties in with this business of rightly relating to each other in the body of Christ, and there has been so much confusion about it lately.

What form of Church government is correct? The Baptists, God love 'em, have a democratic approach where the majority rules. The Presbyterians, God bless them, have elders or presbyters who vote on what's the proper course. The Episcopalians or Catholics have the ascending spiral of authority going higher and higher in the hierarchy, so that when the Pope speaks "from the throne", why that's the last word on it and lo and behold he's "infallible"! So which one's right? The answer is that God is right! The fact is that much of the time the decisions made by all of the aforementioned ways of governing a church can be and have been wrong! (I used to belong to a church where I finally decided that if I flipped a coin, that I would be right a greater percentage of the time than the church leadership. But there is only one government that is correct and always right—-and that is the THEOCRACY!!!

THE THEOCRACY

The Theocracy is always right. But let us define Theocracy. Theocracy = the government of God; The Rulership of God; the Lordship of Jesus Christ; where God is in control. The Kingdom of God is whatever God is the King of!!! The Bible says that, "The earth is the Lord's, and the fullness thereof; the world, and they that dwell therein." (Psalm 24:1) So it all belongs to Him. Yet Jesus Christ says, "Not every one that saith unto Me, 'Lord', 'Lord', shall enter into the Kingdom of Heaven; but he that DOETH the will of My Father which is in heaven." Thus we see that the Theocracy, or the Kingdom of God is what ever God is the King over.

This means then that there is no one who is right or correct, except Jesus Christ, the Holy Spirit, or God the Father, (and those who agree with Him!) God has a right to be right! And we have the right to agree with Him!!! Anyone who disagrees with Him is a Kingdom anarchist, insurrectionist and traitor.

WHAT AND WHEN AND WHERE IS THE KINGDOM OF GOD?

After years of prayer, reading, study, revelation, and experience, we have concluded that THE

KINGDOM OF GOD IS WHAT GOD IS THE KING OF. The Kingdom of God is whatever God is the King over. The Kingdom of God is, the Lordship of Christ is, whatever God or Christ is the boss over.

In other words, if a person invites Christ and God to be the Lord, Chief, Boss, Saviour, Master, Commander, King over his or her life, and lives according to the King's desires, and does what the King wants, then to that extent, that life will be an expression of the Kingdom of God on the earth today.

KINGDOM FAMILY

To the extent that a person (or family) makes God the King over their family, and King over what that wife, husband and children say and do by saying, "God is the King over this family. We shall function under His Lordship, living by His rules and His love, and relate to one another as King Jesus wishes", then to that extent, that family becomes a literal, visible expression of the Kingdom of God! If a person says and does the same thing with his property, possessions, and business, insisting that it be run EXACTLY by the leading of the Holy Spirit (this, of course, necessitates knowing God's voice), then that person's property, possessions, and business becomes a literal, visible demonstration of the Kingdom of God in the right now! This will be a Kingdom family.

A KINGDOM CHURCH

The same principle applies to a church body. If a church decides, REALLY decides to do according to the will of God and the Word of God and the teaching of the Spirit of God, no matter what; worshiping as Christ wants; working, warring as God wants; giving as God wants; being organized as Christ wants; insisting that the ministries and members function and relate to each other and love each other as He wants; then to that same degree and extent that God is King of that congregation, that church will be a living demonstration, in the right now, of the Kingdom of God. This will be a Kingdom Church!

Christ said, "But if I, with the finger of God cast out devils, no doubt the Kingdom of God is come upon you" Luke 11:20 (KJ). And in another place, "The Kingdom of God is within you."

KINGDOM OF GOD

Selected Verses from the New Testament

"But seek ye first the Kingdom of God, and His righteousness; and all these things shall be added unto you." Matt. 6:33. (KJ)

"Or do you not know that the unrighteous shall NOT inherit the Kingdom of God? Do not be deceived: neither fornicators, nor idolators, nor adulterers, nor effeminate, nor homosexuals, nor thieves, nor covetous, nor drunkards, nor revilers, nor swindlers, shall inherit the Kingdom of God." I Cor. 6:9,10.

"Now the works of the flesh are manifest, which are these: adultery, fornication, uncleanness, lasciviousness, idolatry, witchcraft, hatred, variance, emulations, wrath, strife, seditions, heresies, envyings, murders, drunkenness, revellings, and such like: of the which I tell you before, as I have also told you in time past, that they which do such things shall not inherit the Kingdom of God" Gal. 5:19-21 (KJ).

"So that you may walk in a manner worthy of the God who calls you into His own Kingdom and glory. And for this reason we also constantly thank God that when you received from us the word of God's message, you accepted it not as the word of men, but for what it really is, the Word of God, which also performs its work in you who believe" I Th. 2:12,13.

"Now unto the King eternal, immortal, invisible, the only wise God, be honor and glory for ever and ever. Amen" I Tim. 1:17 (KJ).

"And he who overcomes, and he who keeps My deeds until the end, to him I will give authority over the nations; and he shall rule them with a rod of iron, as the vessels of the potter are broken to pieces, AS I also have received authority from My Father" Rev. 2:26,27.

"The kingdoms of this world are become the Kingdoms of our Lord, and of His Christ; and He shall reign for ever and ever" Rev. 11:15 (KJ).

"And she gave birth to a son, a male child, who is to rule all the nations with a rod of iron ..." Rev.12:5.

"....great and marvelous are Thy works, O Lord God, the Almighty; righteous and true are Thy ways Thou King of the nations. Who will not fear, O Lord, and glorify Thy Name? For Thou alone art holy; for all the nations will come and worship before Thee, for Thy righteous acts have been revealed" Rev. 15:3,4.

THE MIGHTY RIGHT NOW GOD!!

Some folks say the Kingdom will be future, or that the Kingdom was past, but some folks like to live in the future or the past. Yahweh means 'The Mighty, RIGHT NOW God.' The Kingdom of God is past or future only to the extent that He was or will be King over something past or future. (And, absolutely He will be King over everything in the future—Everything—EVERY-THING.) Every church, every country, every people, every bank, every political party, every evangelistic association, every denomination, every mission board, every individual shall come under His Kingship or be destroyed. They will come under His rule willingly or unwillingly. "Every knee [shall] bow. and every tongue [shall] confess that Christ Jesus is LORD, to the glory of God the Father" Phil. 2:10,11. "[All] the kingdoms of this world are become the [Kingdom] of our Lord, and of His Christ; and He shall reign for ever and ever" Rev. 11:15 (KJ). This includes every financial kingdom, every religious, every business, every group, every individual kingdom - your kingdom too!

Rom. 14:17 says that the "Kingdom of God is.... righteousness and peace and joy in the Holy Spirit." Do you like that word righteousness? Be honest. Righteousness means rightness—nitty gritty rightness—a right relationship with the King and the citizens of His Kingdom. But, more of this later.

I Cor. 4:20 says that the Kingdom of God consists of power. You'll see what kind of power. You'll either be a channel of it or a victim of it. You'll see just what is the Kingdom of God or the Kingdom of Heaven. Why, it's whatever God is the King of. If you and yours belong completely to the King and live the way He wants, then it's the Kingdom of God. But, if it's not, it's not.

Question: If you are going down the street and the Holy Spirit says, "Turn right", and you keep going straight, is Jesus being your Lord?

Question: If you have a wrong relationship to the King or the citizens of His Kingdom, are you a part of His Kingdom?

The Kingdom of God is what God is King of. Jesus says, "Not everyone that says to Me, 'Lord, Lord' will enter the Kingdom of Heaven, BUT HE THAT DOES THE WILL OF MY FATHER Who is in Heaven" Matt.7:21. Are you one of those who call Him Lord, but do not DO what He says???

Please pray with me, repeating these words with me if you will:

Lord Jesus, I make You King, Lord, and Master of ALL I am and have or ever will have or be. I choose You to be Lord over my possessions, business, family, future, money, my whole life. I give You everything, Everything, EVERYTHING!!! I give You all I am and all that I have and all that I shall ever have or be - IN EXCHANGE FOR all You have and are. From now on Lord God, I want what You want, Your perfect will, no matter what the cost!!! In Jesus' Name, Amen.

HOW DO I JOIN THE KINGDOM OF GOD?

To become a member of the Kingdom of God is extremely simple or difficult, depending on one's perspective. It's easy if a person really wants to walk with God, difficult to the extent one does not. For example, Jesus said, "My yoke is easy, My burden is light." But "The way of the transgressor is hard", and "It is a difficult thing to kick against the ox goad." I've often told folks that if I were to swap all my theology for a totally selfish one, I wouldn't change a thing. Look at these promises from the Bible to a person that is in the will of God:

1— "Joy unspeakable and full of glory" I Pet. 1:8b (KJ).
2— "In Thy presence is fullness of joy; and at Thy right hand there are pleasures for evermore" Ps. 16:11 (KJ).
3— "Life..... abundantly" John 10:10 (KJ).
4— "My joy....in you and your joy.....full" John 15:11.
5— "[The overcomers] shall rule over the nations with a rod of iron" Rev. 2:26,27 (KJ).
6— "God giveth us richly all things to enjoy" I Tim. 6:17 (KJ).
7— "God has blessed us with every spiritual blessing" Eph. 1:3.

.....and infinitely more. Tell me, would you trade any of this for an eternity in hell? But it will cost you. Let's look again to see if the price is worth paying. Jesus Christ asked the question, "What will a man give in exchange for his own soul?" and "What will it profit a man if he gain the whole world and lose his own soul?" (Matt. 16:26; Mark 8:36; Luke 9:25)

Look at the positive side. You want to walk with God. Here's how: First, be born again. In John 3:3,5,7,

Jesus promises that unless you are born again, you cannot see, or enter into, the Kingdom of God. Do you remember that religious painting where Jesus is standing outside the door of the cottage, knocking on the door? You'll see there's no latch on the outside. In Revelation 3:20 Jesus says, "Look, I'm standing at the door of your life and I'm knocking. If any of you will open the door of your life and invite Me to come as your Saviour and Lord, I will come in and we'll have fantastic fellowship together" (JB). You PRAY THIS PRAYER:

"Lord Jesus Christ, I invite You to come in to my life and be all that Your are, in me. I give You my whole life. I admit that I have displeased You many times and have sinned. I receive Your whole Life in exchange for mine and receive You as my Salvation, my Lord, my Life, my Righteousness, etc. I ask You, Heavenly Father, to fill me with Your Holy Spirit of love Always. Thank you, Father for sending Thy Son, Jesus Christ, to take the penalty of my sins for me by dying my death on the cross. I choose to obey You from now on, and to walk close to You, read Your Word, obey You and talk to You often. In Jesus' Name, Amen."

Feel better? You're on your way. John 1:12 is interesting. "But as many as received Him [Christ Jesus], to them [you] gave He the power to become the children of God, even to those who believe in His Name." So the potential to make it big in God is yours. Now, let's see how to make it happen.

HOW TO STAY IN THE KINGDOM OF GOD?!!! OR WHAT IS A CITIZEN OF THE KINGDOM OF GOD?!!

The word of God uses some of the following words to describe a Kingdom citizen: disciples, sons, friends, brothers of Christ, mothers & sisters of Christ. One must pay to become and remain a disciple or member or citizen of God's Kingdom. The cost is: EVERY-THING YOU ARE AND HAVE IN EXCHANGE FOR EVERYTHING GOD HAS AND IS. The only thing that's really required is that one become and DO the will of the Lord. That's the Kingdom of God, simply doing and being what the King wants—the Lordship of Christ.

"As many as are led by the Spirit of God, they are the Sons of God." Rom. 8:14 (KJ). "Not every one that saith unto me, Lord, Lord, shall enter into the Kingdom of heaven; but he that DOETH the will of My Father which is in heaven. Many will say to Me in that day, "Lord, Lord, have we not prophesied in Thy Name? and in Thy Name have cast out devils? and in Thy Name done many wonderful works?' And then I will profess unto them, 'I never knew you: depart from me, ye that work iniquity'" Matt. 7:21-23 (KJ). Jesus asked, "Why call ye me 'Lord', 'Lord', and do not the things which I say?" Luke 6:46 (KJ). Dear one, IT'S NOT ENOUGH to claim to be saved or born again or spirit filled or a church member or anything, if you claim Christ Jesus as your Lord but do not do what he wants or says.

A CITIZEN OF THE KINGDOM OF GOD IS ONE WHO (is born again, but who also) DOES WHAT THE KING OF KINGS, THE LORD JESUS CHRIST WANTS. Let's look at three verses in Luke 14 regarding those who CANNOT be a Kingdom citizen: Large crowds were traveling with Jesus, and turning to them He said: "If anyone comes to Me and does not hate his own father and mother, and wife and children, and brothers and sisters—yes, and even his own life—he CANNOT BE MY DISCIPLE" Luke 14:26-27. What this means simply is that THE WILL OF GOD MUST COME FIRST - ahead of the will, wishes, desires, threats, opinions, commands, or intimidations of your parents, children, spouse, friends, enemies, church members, and those whose opinions you respect the most. MOST OF ALL, the will and desire of God must be surely more important to you than your own will or desire. You MUST carry your cross! But remember Jesus said, "My yoke is easy and My burden is light" Matt. 11:30 (KJ). Which do you choose - your yoke or Satan's yoke, your burden, your friend's burden, or Christ's easy yoke, His light burden? Luke. 14:33, "So therefore, NO ONE OF YOU CAN BE MY DISCIPLE WHO DOES NOT GIVE UP **ALL** HIS OWN POSSES-SIONS"!!! If you want to be His disciple, then you must give up ownership and legal title to EVERY-THING you own—give it to the King of the Kingdom, Jesus Christ and the Father, so that He retains title and ownership to ALL that you have and are! your life! your will! your time! your worship! your children!

164

your spouse! your money! your future! your possessions! your opinions! your plans! your reputation! your career! your sins! your ideas! your religious ruts! your stubbornness! YOURSELF! Unless you are willing to forsake ALL of these things you CANNOT be His disciple!!! It's impossible for you to call Christ Jesus your Lord and do not DO what He wants!!! The Kingdom of God is what God is King of. And if God is not allowed to be your Absolute Master or your King in some area of your life, then it's not the Kingdom of God and you are NOT His brother or disciple or Kingdom citizen or friend. "Ye are my friends IF ye do whatsoever I command you" John 15:14, and, "Why call ye Me, 'Lord', 'Lord', and do not the things which I say?"! Luke 6:46 (KJ).

Jesus said, "NOT everyone that saith unto Me, 'Lord', 'Lord', shall enter into the Kingdom of Heaven; but he that DOETH the will of My Father which is in heaven" Matt. 7:21 (see above). Perhaps you are thinking, "This is impossible." Do you remember Matthew 19:23-26? "Jesus said to His disciples, 'Truly I say to you', [or 'I tell you the truth'], 'it is hard for a rich man to enter the Kingdom of Heaven.' (It still is) 'Again I say to you, it is easier for a camel to go through the eye of a needle than for a rich man to enter the Kingdom of God.' [Think about that!] And when the disciples heard this, they were very astonished and said, 'Then who can be saved?' Jesus [looked at them and] said, 'With men this is impossible, but WITH GOD ALL THINGS ARE POSSIBLE.'" What about it, amigo? Do you want to change the Scriptures to mean, "With God SOME things are possible?", "My God will supply SOME of my needs?", "I can do SOME things through Christ?" But we here are only fulfilling the Great Commission when we are teaching you to OBEY "ALL THINGS WHATSOEVER I (Jesus) have commanded you" Matt. 28:20 (KJ).

Please repeat this prayer with me:

Lord, I repent of my unbelief. I choose to believe in You. I not only seek Your Kingdom first, but also I seek Your righteous - ness. Teach me, Lord Jesus, what seeking first Your righteous - ness is. In Jesus' Name. Amen. And by the way Lord, I now hereby give you Everything I have and am: my life, my will, my time, my worship, my children, my spouse, my money, my future, my possessions, my opinions, my plans, my reputation, my career, my sins, my ideas, my religious ruts, my stubbornness, my self and everything I ever will have or be - NOW! for all time -I give it all to You, forever. In Jesus name, Amen!!!

HEADSHIP and INTIMIDATION

The Kingdom Principle is this: WE MUST ALWAYS BE SUBMISSIVE TO THE CHRIST, THROUGH WHOMEVER HE SPEAKS, AND WHERE EVER HE IS FOUND, EVEN IF HE IS SPEAKING THROUGH A WOMAN, A MAN, A CHILD, OR A DONKEY! (Remember Balaam's donkey.) BUT, WE MUST NEVER BE SUBMISSIVE TO THE OPINION OF MAN, (WHEN THAT OPINION DIFFERS FROM THE OPINION OF

KINGDOM CONTRACT OF TOTAL COMMITMENT TO THE LORD JESUS CHRIST KING OF KINGS AND THE LORD OF LORDS

I hereby totally surrender all that I have and am, or shall ever have or be, completely to Jesus Christ (all other conditions and terms of this contract to be filled in later by the Lord Jesus Christ).

-
-
-
-
-
-
-
-
-
-
-
-
-
-

Date _____

Witness _____GOD_____

Signature _ _ _ _ _ _ _ _ _ _

GOD,) OR TO THE INFLUENCE OF satan, REGARDLESS OF THROUGH WHOM THAT OPINION OR INFLUENCE COMES, EVEN IF IT IS COMING THROUGH THE MIGHTEST APOSTLE! (Remember when Jesus spoke to St Peter and said, "Get thee behind Me, satan !!!)

But there are those within the body of Christ who have other points of view and who in some cases want to "mess with" the Lordship of Jesus Christ as God over people's lives; who want to change the Bible to read: "There are at least TWO mediators, (or 'go betweens') between God and man, the man Christ Jesus PLUS MACHO MAN ME!!!!", instead of the One God, not four or more, and the One Mediator, Jesus Christ, spoken of in 1 Timothy 2. The Book of Revelation describes these types as those who want to "possess men's souls".

Those of us who teach about "headship" need to get our heads straight and teach that Jesus Christ is the Head over all. Well, let's look at it. In Ephesians 5, the Lord says:

"For the husband is head of the wife, even as Christ is the Head of the Church...", but most people that teach about divine order forget that the passage about husbands and wives opens up with the COMMAND, commanding "Submitting yourselves one to another in the fear of God."! and "Husbands, love your wives, even as, (or in the same way that) Christ loved the Church, and gave Himself for it"!!! And how did Christ love the Church??? He washed her feet!!!!!!!! He laid down His life for her! He earnestly intercedes for her before the throne of God! And so ought we to love the woman God gave to us!!! Remember, intimidation and love cannot co-exist. Neither, in the Theocracy of God, (nor in a marriage, or any authority-subordinate relationship), is there room for intimidation, or oppression, or tyranny, or arrogance, or subjugation, or domination, or masochism, or sadism, or torment, or any such thing!!!

SPIRITUAL SADO-MASOCHISM

Let me address just two of these. There are actually those in the body of Christ who seem to have the attitude, "Beat me, humiliate me, punish me, browbeat me, scold me, berate me, belittle me!" They think that good preaching is when they get severely scolded. And there is also another crowd in religious leadership only too willing to oblige!!! We think that this kind of thinking in the world is "sick". And so it is. But it is even sicker in the Church of Jesus Christ! As my friend Wells has pointed out, that in our preaching and ministry there is no room for even a whip made of velvet! I heard one highly respected preacher say to the people, "If you don't stand up and sing, I'm gonna come back there and jerk you out of your seat and make you sing!" (Most of the people laughed.) Much of his preaching has been with the same browbeating and condescending attitude.) So, I wrote him a love letter asking him if he also treated his wife that way in his belligerent intimidation, and gently reminded him that we have no right to intimidate one another in the body of Christ. I wish I could have gotten a thank you letter back from him. Instead, I received severe rejection and railing criticism. Obviously he was not a wise man, for as the Scripture says, "Rebuke a wise man, and he will love thee." I'm still trying to believe, and to get others to believe the Scripture that says, "He that rebuketh a man afterwards shall find more favor than he that flattereth with the tongue." and the one that says, "Open rebuke is better than secret love." (Proverbs, chapters 28 & 27). Will you believe with me? I am really a very gentle person. And, I promise to be teachable if you want to rebuke me!

We will continue to examine our proper relating to each other and to look at authority/subordinate relationships in the next chapter also.

Lord God of the Universe, we ask and believe that You will enable us to always correctly relate to everyone, especially our brothers and sisters in Your Body. In the Mighty Name of Our Lord and Saviour Jesus Christ our Righteousness. Amen.

CHAPTER 8 — REVIEW

1. What form of Church government is correct?
2. Define the word "Theocracy".
3. What is the Kingdom of God? (Briefly)
4. Is the Kingdom of God past, present or future?
5. Even though Jesus told Pilate at the crucifixion, "My Kingdom is not of this world.", Where do the following Scriptures indicate that God's Kingdom is? Psalm 47; Jer. 10:7; Rev.2:26,27; Rev.12:5; Zech. 14:9; Rev.11:15; Rev.l5:3,4 .
6. What percentage would you say that God is King over: a. Your life? b. Your family c. Your job d. Your possessions e. Your church?
7. Would you say that you know the Voice of the Lord? How well do you obey?
8. According to Gal. 5, Eph. 5 and I Cor. 6, make a list of at least 15 kinds of people, or things that people do that will cause them to be excluded from the Kingdom of God.
9. According to Rev. 2:26,27, who will have authority over the nations and who will rule them with a rod of iron?
10. List specifically some of the kinds of kingdoms that will either become the Kingdom of our Lord or be destroyed.
11. Make a guess (no answer will be provided by the teacher at this time) as to who the manchild is in Rev.l2:5.
12. What is the meaning of the word YAHWEH?

13. What four things does Rom. 14:17 and I Cor. 4:20 say the Kingdom of God consists of?

14. Is Jesus being your Lord if you turn left when the Holy Spirit says "Go straight" or "Turn right"?

15. Is Jesus being your King if you have a wrong relationship to His subjects?

16. If you call Jesus your Lord, but don't do what the Father wants — will you inherit the Kingdom of God? (Matt. 7:21).

17. Have you given or will you give yourself to Jesus Christ now 100%?

18. Along with all that you own?; a. Or will ever own?; b. Or all that you are; c. Or will ever be?.

19. Explain what it means by being "born again"? (John 3:3,5,7)

20. How long have you been born again?

21. Who was instrumental in your new birth?

22. Why no latch on the outside of the door where Jesus is knocking?

23. If we open the door to our heart and invite Christ to come in, what will happen?

24. When Christ comes in, does He come in as Guest, Roomer, or Total Lord and Master of all the house?

25. How much does it cost to join the Kingdom of God?

26. List at least 12 things that we get in exchange.

27. Can we know that we are saved?

28. Who is our Salvation? (Not what, but Who?)

29. Is salvation a crisis or a process?

30. Does "Works" have anything to do with our salvation? Eph.2:8-10.

31. How many productive years do you think you have left before you stand before the judgment seat of Christ?

32. What is the first thing necessary to become a citizen of the Kingdom of God?

33. Give at least 4 synonyms the Lord gives for a Kingdom citizen.

34. What one single characteristic marks or identifies a born again citizen of the Kingdom of God?

35. How much does it cost to be a citizen of the Kingdom of God?

36. Is it possible to claim Jesus as Lord and still not inherit the Kingdom of God? (Read Rom.8:14; Matt.7:21-23; Lk.6:46 and write them down.)

37. What two groups of people did Jesus say cannot be His disciples? (Lk.14:26-27)

38. Lk.14:33 says who else cannot be Christ's disciple?

39. What generally & specifically must we give up? (Make a list of at least 12 things)

40. What general & specific things are you willing to give to Him now 100%? (List at least 30 things)

41. What generally & specifically are you willing to do for the Lord Jesus Christ? (List at least 30 things)

42. What generally & specifically are you willing to be for the Lord Jesus Christ? (List at least 12 things)

43. If you are not Christ's disciple — then whose disciple are you?
44. Will it be harder or more difficult to be Christ's disciple or the devil's. (Guess) Rom. 8:18, Prov. 13:15, Matt. 11:28-29.
45. What of ours did Christ take with Him to the cross? (Name at least 3 of the most important things.)
46. Is it necessary for us to "feel" saved before we are?
47. What verse proceeds the verse, "For the husband is head of the wife..." from Epesians 5?
48. Complete the statement, "Intimidation and love cannot _____ ".
49. Define "spiritual masochism".

Chapter 9 - Outline
WHEN IT'S WISE TO CRITICIZE
or
KINGDOM PROTOCOL
or
SANCTIFIED CRITICISM

I. Know Right By Noting Wrong

II. Sanctified Rebellion

III. Subordination Vs Submission

IV. The Golden Rule Of Submission

V. The Vision Of The Four "Horses"

VI. Timbuck Or Podunk

VII. "Light In The Closet"

VIII. Tuff Love

IX. Have Nothing To Do With Them

X. Sex

XI. Drugs

Some Selected Scriptures

"After you have removed the beam that is in your own eye, then go and remove the speck that is in your brother's eye." Jesus. Lk.6.

"If your brother offends you, rebuke him, and if he repents, forgive him." (Forgive him any way) Jesus, from Luke 17:3.

"Rebuke not an elder but GO TO HIM, AND PLEAD WITH HIM AS A SON TO A FATHER." I Tim.5:1.

"If we walk in the light as He is in the light, we have fellowship with one another, and the blood of Jesus Christ cleanses us from ALL sin." I John 1:7

Proverbs 27:5 & 6, "Open rebuke is better than secret love (or a deceitful friendship)" "Better are the wounds of a friend, than the kisses of an enemy."

Proverbs 27:17, "As iron sharpens iron, so the countenance of a man his friend."

Proverbs 28:23, "He who rebukes a man shall find more favor afterwards than he who flatters with his tongue."

"If you are in the process of giving your gift at the altar, and you remember that your brother has something against you, leave your gift at the altar (ungiven) and go to your neighbor, make it right, and then come and present your gift." Jesus, Mat. 5:23-24.

9

WHEN IT'S WISE TO CRITICIZE
or
KINGDOM PROTOCOL

Know Right By Noting Wrong

There are actually those in the body of Christ that teach the following:

1. They think THAT "You are 'poz to do what the elders, or the Pope, or the pastor, or the husband, or the parent, or the government, say for you to do, without question." Sound like Jim Jones? The truth is, that no one has the right to cross another person's conscience, or demand that another be submissive to something for which they do not have faith. (Rom. 14).

2. They think THAT "you are absolved from responsibility for your actions when you are acting in submission to authority!" Sound like Hitler? Acts 4:19 and other Scriptures indicate that we shall give an awesome responsibility at the judgement seat of Christ for what we do or say!

179

3. They think THAT "passive, killed spirit, plough horse submission is the ideal". Sound "macho"? No, God wants us to be effervescent and buoyant and creative and aggressive and dynamic in our submission!

4. They think THAT "if you get a 'leading' contrary to the 'leading' of the authority, that you "jes' pos' keep yo mouf shet n' gwine do it." Sound prejudiced? With a right spirit, the subordinate has not only the privilege, but also the responsibility to voice what that one believes to be the will of God. ALSO, the leadership has the awesome responsibility to harken carefully to counsel coming through subordinate channels lest they fail to hear the voice of the Lord speaking through the one in the place of lesser authority. Bible says, "A little child shall lead them." Isa.11:6.

5. They think THAT "the person in authority is superior to the one in the subordinate position". (For example, that the wife is inferior to the husband.) Sound chauvinistic? The story of Nabal, David & Abigail in the Old Testament is really beautiful here. There is no question as to who had the superior wisdom, actions, decisions, beauty, and worth in the eyes of God and man. (1 Samuel 25.)

6. They think THAT "50 million bishops, (or Frenchmen, or cemetary graduates or Baptists, or charismatics, or rupturists, or infernal securitists, or anti-charismatics, or whatever), can't be wrong". The true fact of the matter is that almost without exception, the majority is wrong the majority of the

180

time!! That is, majority opinion mostly, is or has been wrong the majority of the time. I have actually seen some ideal church situations, where they had apostles, prophets, evangelists, pastors, teachers, elders, deacons, deaconesses, intercessors, givers, administrators, miracle workers and helps, where the individual seeking counsel would have been right a greater percentage of the time by flipping a coin, as a means of determining the right course of action, than to commit his entire destiny into the hands of these austere ministries and blindly following them. It is amazing to me how many people can "get the word of the Lord" for others, that don't know, or do, the will of God for themselves!

Please understand, we BELIEVE that a church should have apostles, prophets, elders, pastor and deacons, etc. But we also believe that everyone should be led by God, and NOT by some-one-important-else contrary to the will of God!!!

But in order to do right and to be right, we must be dedicated to live uncompromisingly under the Lordship of Jesus Christ and the Leadership of the Holy Spirit, no matter who or what or how many dear ones say or try to influence to the contrary. Believe it or not, there is sometimes danger in numbers. And as we say in another place, if a person has a sell-out price, satan is sure to come up with the silver. The worst prostitution of all is that religious prostitution that compromises the will of God in order to obtain, gain, or maintain favor in the eyes of men.

The Bible says that "In the multitude of counsellors there is safety." Proverbs 11:14. But it also gives a multitude of concrete examples where the majority of and the most notable authority of counsellors was wrong. The right course is one that stands totally committed to the perfect will of God without compromise, drawing on those within the Body of Christ for CONFIRMATION. If someone comes to me and asks me what the will of God is in their situation, I almost always ask them what THEY believe the will of God is for their situation. If they have not first prayed through to a place of inner knowing for themselves, I refuse to protract their spiritual infancy, or to cultivate an over-dependence on me. Instead, I send them back to the Lord Jesus for Him to tell them what to do. Only then am I available for confirmation. The Bible does NOT say, "Work out somebody else's salvation with fear and trembling"!

7. Other religious leaders think THAT "the Bible closes with an awesome thud after the solemn and religious reading of, 'REBUKE NOT AN ELDER'"!! The sad joke is that people do not realize that the verse does not end there, but continues on without pause and says, "BUT GO TO HIM and PLEAD WITH HIM AS A SON TO A FATHER"!!! I Tim.5:1. The Body Of Christ would be much more healthy if people would go to their pastor with their input, lists, criticisms and suggestions, instead of cannibalistically having roast preacher for dinner or voting him out at the next "bored" meeting, or on the other hand, of

glibly, blindly, automatically swallowing and following, just because someone says or does so.

Remember: WE MUST ALWAYS BE SUBMISSIVE TO THE CHRIST, THROUGH WHOMEVER HE SPEAKS, AND WHERE EVER HE IS FOUND, EVEN IF HE IS SPEAKING THROUGH A WOMAN, A CHILD, A DONKEY, OR A MAN. (Remember Balaam's donkey), BUT WE MUST NEVER BE SUBMISSIVE TO THE INFLUENCE OF satan, OR THE OPINION OF MAN (WHEN IT IS CONTRARY TO THE WILL OF GOD), REGARDLESS OF THROUGH WHOM THAT INFLUENCE OR OPINION COMES, (EVEN IF IT IS COMING THROUGH THE MIGHTIEST APOSTLE)!!!

RIGHTEOUS REBELLION & SANCTIFIED INSURRECTION
or
SUBORDINATION vs SUBMISSION

The following are all Scriptural examples of Godly "rebellion" that had the favor and approval of God, (or of 'submission' that did not)! Please note the difference between being subordinate and being submissive. For example, Moses was subordinate to God, but in this case was not submissive, though he was the "meekest man on the face of the earth."

SANCTIFIED REBELLION

1. Exodus 32. The people "mess up". God says, "Stand aside Moses. I'm going to kill all these people, and make of you a mighty nation." Moses said, "Lord

NO, I WON'T go. You're NOT going to kill all of these people. You're NOT going to make a nation out of me. I'm NOT going to stand aside. And if You do kill them, You can kill me right along with them." And then, believe it or not, (look it up if you want to), the Bible says, "And the Lord repented of the evil which He thought to do unto His people." !!!

Lord,I wish there were more ministries that would do the same! I believe it to be, in Jesus Christ's Name! 'Cause I don't want us to stand in shame. I don't want us to be to blame. For these reasons the Spirit's flame Has illumined the Word that came.

This happened again in Numbers 14:12. But the sad fact is, that there was no one stood "in the gap" for Moses when he "messed up", although he did finally get to go into the Promised Land!!! (Matthew 17). I dare YOU to argue with God like that!

2. Jacob fighting with Jesus Christ! (Genesis 32). The Lord said, "Let Me go!" Jacob said, "Lord, no!, except You do what I say!" To which the Lord replied, "O.K., have it your way. You win!" I dare YOU to argue (and wrestle) with God like that.

3. Ruth being 'unsubmissive' to Naomi. Ruth chapter 1. Four times, Naomi told Ruth to turn back. Ruth refused, and was rewarded. She became the grandmother of King David, and the ancestor of Jesus.

4.Joseph refused to 'submit' to his employer. (Genesis 39.)

5. Abigail went contrary to her husband's wishes and was rewarded. In fact, God killed him and gave

184

her a new husband who would do the will of God! (1 Samuel 25). No divorce necessary here!

6. David had to 'fight' his older brothers for the privilege of doing the will of God! (1 Samuel 17). He exercised initiative totally alone and on his own, except for the help of God. Only after he was successful in his venture, then finally every one else decided to get on the band wagon. Talk about a moral minority!

7. Jonathan, acting contrary to his father's wishes, only with the help of a single friend and the help of God acted entirely alone and was totally responsible in God for the winning of the war, only to be sentenced to death for his accomplishments!!! (I Samuel 13). Where are the Jonathans and the Armor bearers today? Where are today's giant killers who will fly in the face of immoral majority? Who will dare to do mighty exploits in the Name of a Mighty God and bring mighty glory to Him?!!. It is obvious from these and a host of other illustrations that sometimes it is necessary for us to fight for the privilege of doing the will of God, and that sometimes we must fight, or at least go against the wishes of, those closest to us.

8. Elisha repeatedly refused to submit to his master's demands and was rewarded with a double portion because of it! (II Kings 2:2,4,6).

9. The young miracle-working prophet became submissive to the old prophet. As a result, God killed him dead. (Read it, it says, and I quote: "GOD - KILLED - HIM - DEAD!" v.26) (Aren't you glad that

Jesus Christ is the same, yesterday, today and forever!) Suppose the "ministries" want you to be submissive to Plan A, but you believe that God wants you to be submissive to Plan B. Believe it or not, there are those in the body of Christ who teach that you should be submissive to Plan A, and that God will bless you for going contrary to your leading, your conviction and your conscience!!! If you are ever in this situation, please be reminded to read, and heed again the story of the Old Prophet VS. the Young Prophet in 1 Kings (unlucky) 13! For those of you who are wondering if I am advocating irresponsible anarchy or a spastic independence, please stay with me, because I am advocating the Theocracy of God, The Lordship of Jesus Christ, and the Leadership of the Holy Spirit. I promise to explain how this works out on a practical level. I know that we gave this example before, but it is interesting to note that even in situations where a person decides for himself the will of God, even by guessing or flipping a coin, (we are not recommending this), one often hits the will of God more often than in many situations where there is benefit of oppressive religious leadership that has protracted infancy and stymied growth by creating an unhealthy dependency on "headship". People in that place most often lose their initiative to press in to know the Voice of the Lord and the Mature Leading of God for their own lives, because the "leadership" has become their "lord", instead of the Lord Jesus Christ!

10. Balaam's ass. Numbers 22 tells the story of the prophet whose donkey refuses to go where his master wants because the donkey sees grave danger for his master that the prophet does not see! Let all of those who are in leadership, or who will be, to have godly fear and godly trembling, lest you also fail hear the Lord speaking to you through what you consider to be a jack-ass or a bohlen-ball! And to those of you who are considered to be as donkeys in the house of God, or have come to think this of yourself, be encouraged! If God could speak through a donkey, then He can speak through you!! It's your privilege. It's your responsibility!!! In fact, we encourage you to, with a right spirit, practice on your spiritual leaders and your spiritual headship. They need the practice too, of listening with a right spirit to Christ speak to them through subordinate channels! The Bible says that "a little child shall lead them", and sometimes a jackass will too! God grant that they and we will all have ears to hear what the Spirit has to say to us, through WHOMEVER He chooses! Do I hear an "Amen" from the leaders?

11. The little maid, in II Kings chapter 5, was only a little maid. (Makes sense, doesn't it?) What would have happened if the big-important-great-mighty-honorable-captain-man had not listened to the counsel of this lowly maid??? The same thing would have happened as has in fact happened to many ministries and churches that have refused to listen to the lowly little maids through whom the Lord Jesus

Christ speaks: the spiritual leprosy has continued. (Doesn't make sense does it?)

12. Daniel refused to submit to the governmental leadership though it meant the lion's den. (Daniel 6) The plotters were killed by their own plot, by their own lions, in their own den They were measured and "meated" by their own measure!!! And, the Gospel was taken to the whole world!!!

13. The three refused to submit to the king's edict though it meant being thrown into the furnace of fire! (Daniel 3). Talk about a meeting with the Lord! The people who threw them in got burned instead and the Gospel was taken to the whole world!

14. Acts 21 tells where Paul refused to be submissive to the church or the ministries who got repeated witness by the Holy Spirit not to go to Jerusalem, (vss.4-14), yet he had been clearly told by the Holy Spirit to go! (20:22). The fantastic lesson here is that of verse 14, "And when he would not be persuaded, we ceased, saying, 'the will of the Lord be done' "! No psychic intimidation, no "Christian" witchcraft here! They just lovingly commended him to the grace of God. And unless the Bible has clearly indicated that the person is DEFINITELY SINNING, we must also lovingly commend each other to the grace of God, accepting Jesus as their Lord also, and withholding criticism. Here also is an excellent example of the need for the wisdom to apply the knowledge, for it is not enough to know the facts, as both the prophet AND Paul did, but God's wisdom, in properly handling that knowledge, is also necessary.

15. Peter and the other apostles blatantly refused to be submissive to the high priest, the captain of the temple, the chief priests, the council, the established religious leadership of that day!!! (Acts 5).

16. Jesus ignored a poor woman and then called her a dog even after the disciples all VOTED to reject her. They had a quorum, a majority. It was unanimous. How would you have reacted? What would you have done? She still persisted, still maintained her faith, still kept a right spirit!!! Yet in her rightness of heart, she argued with the Lord Jesus Christ, the Creator King of All the Universe, and got the happy answer to her prayer plus the congratulations of the Lord!!! (Matthew 15 & Mark 7).

17. Paul publicly withstood the Apostle Peter to his face because of Peter's sin. (Galatians 2).

THE GOLDEN RULE OF SUBMISSION

"WE MUST ALWAYS BE SUBMISSIVE TO THE CHRIST WHEREVER HE IS FOUND OR THROUGH WHOMEVER HE IS SPEAKING, (even if He is speaking through a donkey,) BUT WE MUST NEVER BE SUBMISSIVE TO THE OPINIONS OF MAN (CONTRARY TO THE WILL OR WORD OF GOD), OR THE INFLUENCE OF satan, REGARDLESS OF THROUGH WHOM THAT INFLUENCE/OPINION COMES, (even if it's through the mightiest apostle.)!!!"

Please be patient with us here, because we will show very clearly what the Lord Jesus teaches in this regard.

189

When, then, are we to be submissive to those who are "over us in the Lord" or to those who have spiritual authority??? Please hear me to the end of the paragraph...The answer is NEVER - YET we are to ALWAYS be submissive to the Lord Jesus Christ through whomever He speaks and wherever He is found!!! Let me illustrate. Please look at the record of Matthew sweet 16. Jesus asks His disciples who they think that He is. They toss around their human guesstimation. Finally Peter comes up with the right answer and Christ tells him that he really "done" good, and sends him to the head of the class with the keys to the door. But just a few verses later Jesus does something really really interesting! (Doesn't He always?!) "But He turned, and said unto Peter, "Get thee behind Me, satan: thou art an offense unto Me: for thou savorest not the things that be of God, but those that be of men." Sometimes we must be lovingly "stern" with each other as Jesus was here with His friend Peter.

Notice here that Jesus does not accuse Peter of being "devil possessed" but says "get behind me Satan, because Peter, you are thinking like a human." The carnal mind is "emnity against God", and "The natural man receiveth not the things of the Spirit of God: for they are foolishness unto him: neither can he know them, because they are spiritually discerned." I Cor.2:14. And when the mightiest apostle gives us his best "human" advice today, we are under no obligation to be submissive, if he is speaking contrary to the will and Word of God!. In fact, we are obligated to be submissive to the Lord every time His desire for us differs from our own or any one else!!! Any one.

THE VISION OF THE FOUR 'HORSES'

Visualize with me four different horse-like creatures, each symbolic of one who is to be subordinate. The first is a magnificent winged beauty wild and free, standing on the edge of the mountain. Fire comes out from under its feet when she prances, and from her mouth when she speaks. With head and tail held high, its muscles ripple and her mane flies in the wind.

The second creature is the same as the first, except that she has been captured and caged and her spirit has been broken. She sprawls sadly and stupidly in the middle of the corral, her crown taken and her wings broken. Its back is sagging and head, mane and tail hang down; her eyes are blinded and the fire is out.

The third creature is like the first and second, captured and caged, but she refuses to be submissive or subordinate, cooperative or willing. This creature is rebellious and stubborn, brawling and contentious, using her fire and feet destructively. She is good for nothing but to be turned loose or shot, the symbol of rebellion.

The fourth creature is identical to the first in every way, except that she is proudly pulling the chariot of God the King. She was in the corral for a moment. But she eagerly wanted to co-operate and be a part of things, no longer lonely or alone. She exchanged one kind of freedom for another and has no regrets. She still has her wings, her sight, her zeal, her fire and her effervescence. She is moving the direction the rider wants her to go before he is firmly settled in the saddle. All who see her wonder at the One with whom she is associated.

The first creature is a picture of UNTESTED SUBMISSION. There are those who have had the good sense to come out, but don't have enough sense to come in and be "set in to the Body of Christ as it pleases Him"! They have not known the test of the desert, the crucible or the cross (or the resurrection!), so they have not yet passed the test. They have not known the fire that purifies the gold, so they have not yet come forth as gold..

The second is a picture of PLOW-HORSE, KILLED SPIRITED SUBMISSION, PASSIVE & BLIND. Her creativity, initiative and motivation are gone. She has been psychically emasculated and disemboweled, yet she lives. The Bible says, "Let no man take thy crown." Someone else said, "If you do, they will!" Bible says, "Stand fast in the liberty wherewith Christ has set you free, and be not entangled again in the yoke of bondage." Revelation 18 speaks unkindly about those who possess or make merchandise of the "souls of men."

The third creature is a type of REBELLION. She is stubborn and un-cooperative. It is the 'old maid' of the pop-corn pot, (we are not speaking of un-married ladies), the "grain of wheat" that "refuses to fall into the ground and die". God says, "For rebellion is as the sin of witchcraft, and stubbornness is as iniquity and idolatry. Because thou hast rejected the Word of the Lord, He hath also rejected thee..." I Samuel 16:23

The fourth creature is a type of AGGRESSIVE CREATIVE BUOYANT EFFERVESCENT DYNAMIC MAJESTIC OVERFLOWING MAGNIFICENT SUBMISSION!

TIMBUCK & PODUNK
or
THE LIGHT IN THE CLOSET

Look at this illustration if you will. Suppose there is husband and wife who are each seeking the Lord in their respective prayer closets. While they are praying, let's say that the Lord simultaneously speaks to both of them an opposite thing, telling the husband, "Thou shalt move with thy family to Podunk." But to the wife the Lord says, "Thou shalt move with thy family to Timbuck"! First of all, could such a thing be? Anyway, back to the closet, let's say this is what happens, and that when it happens, they both get excited that God spoke to them and that they can't wait to tell their spouse the news. The closet doors burst open and they come running into each others arms and say to each other, "God spoke to me!" So 'macho man' speaks first. He forgot the lady is supposed to go first. "God spoke to me that we are to move to Podunk, let's pack our bags!"

Suppose she is like rebellious creature #3 above. Now please note that there is no association between a wife and a horse intended, as we are likening these creatures to all subordinates in any subordinate-

193

authority relationship such as student-teacher, employee-employer, child-parent, people-pastor, wife-husband, man-God kinds of relationships. But if the wife is like the rebellious creature, her response to her husband will be, "Heck no, I won't go!" If she is like #2 creature, her response will be, "O.K. Anything you say. Just hit me with a stick, and we'll be on our way." There are many groups that really do believe this dead submission is the same as that taught in the New Testament! Some people actually think, or try to get others to think that this is the kind of submission that they are to have to the elders or pastor, or that the wife's submission to her husband should be this kind of Second Creature: Passive, killed spirit plow horse submission, without question, objection or discussion. But, this passive kind of blind submission is never ever Ever taught in the word of God, for ANY authority-subordinate relationship!!! Suppose that the parent tells the child not to get out of bed after bed-time and the house catches fire? Suppose the major tells the private "attention" but a truck is about to hit the major? Suppose a policeman tells a person to stop running when the runner knows that a bomb will explode in two seconds? Suppose a teacher will not allow a child to leave class, when there really IS an unexplainable personal emergency?

In this Podunk-Timbuck illustration, suppose the wife is like the fourth effervescent creation. She will perhaps quietly say, "And now darling, please let me share with you what I believe the Lord has shown me." The "plow-horse" would have been thinking, "I must be submissive to my husband, it's his job to get the revelation, and mine to follow, his to command, mine to blindly obey. Therefore, I must not say anything, but just meekly do." The lying line of teaching here is that "if the husband is wrong, God will make everything o.k. and will vindicate the wife without her saying anything." But this is wrong thinking, wrong doing and wrong teaching. In other words, passive, killed-spirited, blind, plow-horse submission is WRONG!

One fellow, a friend of mine, was actually heard to remark, "You know, it was actually a revelation to me that my wife had been given to me by God to be more than a cleaner of my dirty house, (floors, bathrooms,) my dirty dishes, my dirty clothes, my dirty kids," (some men could add, "and my dirty dog")!!! "It was new to me the thought that God had also given her to me to be a help to me in wise counsel and the things of the Holy Spirit!!!"

So, to the extent that the wife is aggressively submissive, she will see that it is her obligation and privilege to share what God is revealing to her about the matter. But suppose the husband is a macho-arrogant-demanding-domineering-belligerent-bully, (qualities that all too well also describe too many people in positions of authority). Suppose he responds by saying, "Look, woman, I'm the boss. You 'pos' do what I say! Now get to packing!" (Would you blame her if she did?)

But instead, she is aggressively submissive and insists on the right to share, and thus she shares,

"Sweetheart, I will go pack, and with a right spirit, but first let me say that if you persist in your stubbornness, that God Himself will spank or judge you and since I don't really want to see this happen, I plead with you to listen to what well may be the voice of the Lord speaking through me!

Assume for a moment that he listens and is even willing to go back into the prayer closet before the Lord. When he does, God speaks to him one of the following things: 1. God may say, "Husband, you are right. In fact, you are both right! I gave to the more practical of you the name of the place to which you will be moving first, and I gave to the more visionary of you the name of the place where you will eventually go in the fulfillment of My plan for you."

Or, God may say, (boss-man, really try to use your imagination here,) "You are wrong and your wife is right. You had the number of syllables in the name of the town correct, the reason for the move, the right direction, and proper timing. But, because you once knew a town by that name and not the name of the other, you incorrectly assumed...!"

So, we see that any one of the following combinations may have been possible:

1. Podunk first, move to Timbuck second. (Both are right.)
2. Timbuck first, move to Podunk second. (Both are right.)
3. Podunk only - (Husband is right, wife mistaken.)

4. Timbuck only - (Wife is right, husband mistaken.)

5. Neither, - (Both were mistaken.)

But suppose the husband is steadfastly stubborn, arrogantly demanding, and pompously belligerent, (God forbid!). Says the tyrant, "Hey stupid, you pack our bags 'fore I hit you up long side 'jo haid!" If she then keeps a right spirit, God will do one of the following things:

1. God will change the husband for her sake.

2. God will change the circumstances for her sake.

3. God may, if the husband continues his tyrannical stupidity, kill the husband and replace him with a man who will do the will of God!!! The story of Abigail and Nabal in I Samuel 25 is a classic example of this last point. God doesn't believe in divorce, but He sure has allowed a lot of people to be killed who stand in the way of His Plan, Will and Purpose. Are you willing to pray this prayer? Please do!

"Dear Lord God, Awesome Judge of all the Universe, Please get glory to Yourself as much as is supernaturally possible, through my life. And if You can't get glory from my life, please change me so that You can! And if You can't change me Lord, then please kill me, and raise up someone else that You can get glory from!"

So also, there are those in positions of authority in the Church, and elsewhere who misuse their authority. To these, God gives a promise: "And I will set up shepherds over them which shall feed them: and they shall fear no more, nor be dismayed, neither

197

shall they be lacking, saith the Lord." Jeremiah 23:4. The Bible promises that God is taking over, and that His Theocracy shall be established in the earth, and that nothing shall stand against it, and that everything that tries shall be destroyed. Rev.11:15.

Thus, it is the privilege, yea, the responsibility of those who are in subordinate positions, when they disagree with those who are in a God chosen place of authority 'over' them, to voice that disagreement to the authority itself, (NOT to someone else), and say, "Brother, (or sister), I love you. I honor your place in God. But I plead with you as a son to a father. I believe that you are wrong, wrong, wrong, wrong, wrong, wrong, wrong. And I plead with you that you get on your face before God until you are right in this matter." If your leader will not listen to you with a right spirit; and if he will not at least get on his face before the Lord in the matter, then we are recommending that you ask God to make your leaders teachable. If they refuse to change, ask God to give you to those who ARE AND WILL BE teachable, entreatable, approachable, and talk-with-able. Remember though, that they are not obligated to do what you think they should. You may be the one who is mistaken! But they, and ALL OF US, ARE RESPONSIBLE TO LISTEN CAREFULLY WITH GODLY FEAR, LEST WE FAIL TO HEAR THE VOICE OF THE LORD SPEAKING THROUGH THE SUBORDINATE VESSEL. If your leader will not at least listen, unless you are married to him, get another leader.

198

Remember, then, the Kingdom Principle: WE MUST ALWAYS BE SUBMISSIVE TO THE CHRIST WHERE EVER HE IS FOUND OR THROUGH WHOMEVER HE IS SPEAKING, EVEN IF IT'S THROUGH A WOMAN, A CHILD, A DONKEY, OR A MAN. BUT WE MUST NEVER BE SUBMISSIVE TO THE INFLUENCE OF satan OR HUMAN OPINION THAT IS CONTRARY TO GOD, REGARDLESS OF THROUGH WHOM THAT INFLUENCE OR OPINION COMES — EVEN IF THAT INFLUENCE IS COMING THROUGH THE MIGHTIEST APOSTLE. (Most of you don't even KNOW any apostles, and some don't even know that they exist - so you don't have anything to worry about).

TOUGH LOVE

God has given us some really clear, simple and beautiful directions for getting along within the Body of Christ. But all of these directions may be reduced to one little word....(LOVE)!

But first let us deal with some practical, gut-level times when the command of God is to allow His love to be manifested through "tough-love". God says, "Those who I love, I rebuke and chasten."

HAVE NOTHING TO DO WITH THEM?

There are some very important Scriptures (aren't they all) that tell us to not associate with certain ones in the Body of Christ. Notice: we are not to draw the circle tighter than God on the one hand, nor yet make the circle looser than God on the other. Nothing is said about separation over the the "faith move" or "tongues" or "manifested sons", but the list is very clear, and by the way, very short!!! Please notice:

Romans 16:17 - "Now I beseech you, brethren, mark THEM WHICH CAUSE DIVISIONS ...and avoid them." Do you know anybody like this?

I Corinthians 5:11 & 13b, "But now I have written unto you not to keep company, if any man (or woman) that is called a BROTHER, (or sister), be a FORNICATOR, or COVETOUS, or an IDOLATOR, or a RAILER, (one who "bad mouth's" people), or a DRUNKARD, or EXTORTIONER; with such an one no, NOT TO EAT...therefore PUT AWAY FROM AMONG YOURSELVES that wicked person."

II Thessalonians 3, "Now we command you, brethren in the Name of our Lord Jesus Christ, that ye withdraw yourselves from every brother that walketh disorderly,...working not at all...IF ANY WOULD NOT WORK, neither should he eat...and if any man obey not our word by this Epistle, note that man, and HAVE NO COMPANY WITH him, that he may be ashamed. Yet count him not as an enemy, but admonish him as a brother." (verses 6a, 10b, 11b, 14b, & 15).

I Timothy 6:3-5, "These things teach and exhort. If any man teach otherwise, and consent not to wholesome words, even the words of our Lord Jesus Christ, and to the doctrine which is according to godliness; he is PROUD; knowing nothing, but doting about questions and strifes of words, whereof cometh

Envy, STRIFE, RAILINGS, EVIL SURMISINGS, PERVERSE DISPUTINGS of men of corrupt minds,...SUPPOSING THAT GAIN IS GODLINESS: FROM SUCH WITHDRAW THYSELF."

Matthew 18:15-17, "If thy brother shall trespass against thee, go and tell him (NOT SOMEBODY ELSE!), his fault between thee and him alone: if he shall hear thee, thou hast gained thy brother." "But if he will not hear thee, then take with thee one or two more, that in the mouth of two or three witnesses every word may be established." "And if he shall neglect to hear them, tell it unto the church: but if he neglect to hear the church, let him be unto thee as an heathen man and a publican."

These are our Redeemer's Rules of Rightly Relating to one another. They may all be summed up in one word - LOVE!!!!!

But it is not to be a theoretical love, (there is no such thing).

The reason that God has established these rules is not because He is either "legalistic" or "religious", but because He really does have our best interest in mind. By "religious" here, we mean "as opposed to being spiritual". For example, it is possible to be religious in the sense of going through the motions, yet not be "for real" spiritually speaking. Yet it is possible to be deeply spiritual and "for real", and yet not appear to be "religious". By "legalistic", we mean, "to be locked into the 'letter' of the law without being locked into the true 'spirit' and intent behind the law. For example, the 'law' said to stone the woman taken in adultery, yet Jesus forgave her and told her not to sin any more. John 8:3-12.

SEX

Permit me to take just a moment to explain, at least partially, why God is so against sex with anyone other than your spouse.

The playboy philosophy has it that "sex need mean no more than shaking hands". Both go their separate ways and that's it. The Bible shows the prostitute's attitude to be not much different. It says, "...she wipeth her mouth, and saith, 'I have done no wickedness'." Proverbs 30:20b. But the Scripture indicates that there are literally terrifying implications and hideous happenings when one has sex with someone they are not married to!!! In I Corinthians 6 the Lord says that we "Become one flesh" or "ONE NATURE" with the sexual partner. Here, and in many other places, God makes clear that it is like taking a half glass of water and half a glass of some other fluid: milk, sewage, vomit, pus or what ever and pouring them back and forth until they are totally and inextricably intermingled. The glass containers represent the person's body, and the liquid represents all that the person is: their mind, will, emotions, thinking, character, spirit and soul. When a person has sex with someone, all that they are becomes totally intermingled with all that the other person is. This is one of the main reasons God commands us not to have sex with anyone other than the one to whom we are married, and explains one reason why there is so much suicide and mental problems among the promiscuous. In the Body of Christ, the implications are even more astounding because when we accept Christ within, to be our Saviour, Lord and LIFE, then the members of our body become the members of Christ Jesus. And if we then commit fornication or adultery, it is like forcing Christ into a rape situation. The reason God is so concerned for us in this area is His concern for His Body-His Beloved Bride that she not become contaminated by "Typhoid-Mary" types. Because we are so closely attuned to one another, the Lord wants us not to be contaminated and thus commands us to be pure and to not associate with anyone in the Body of Christ who is an adulterer or fornicator. Instead, they are to be placed "under quarantine" for their own good and ours, until deliverance and repentance occurs.

DRUGS

The same thing is true of drugs and alcohol, (which is also a drug). The greek word used in the Bible for witchcraft and sorcery is "pharmakeia" from which we get our word "pharmacy" or "pharmaceutical", etc. The reason for this is that devil worship and witchcraft has almost always included the use of various kinds of drugs. The reason for this is that drugs act upon the human soul and spirit so as to disintegrate, dissolve and weaken one's natural resistance to a free invasion of the negative realm of spirit, or evil spirits. Some individuals who have the ability to "see in the spirit" can actually see this disintegration take place, and it apparently looks as if one were pouring hot water on a thin sheet of ice, or acid on a thin sheet of metal.

For example, in a burn accident, we are told that usually the biggest problem is not the burn itself, but infection which results from the destruction of the natural protective covering of the skin, which normally acts as a buffer against the free invasion of negative germs and virus. So, also in the ingestion of drugs and alcohol to excess, when this God given immunity to evil spirits is taken away, or is weakened, there takes place then this free invasion of evil spirits, who forge chains and build landing strips that continue after the drug has "worn off".

There are those who joke about drunks who see pink elephants or drug users and their "hallucinations", but its a bad sad joke because many times, that which drug users see, while under the influence, and subsequently, is real!!! I believe that if we could see in the spirit realm, (and some of us can), most bars would look like the tavern scene from Star Wars. Remember, the realm of spirit both good and bad, is more real than the natural world we see with natural eyes.

Can you see now why God has pleaded with us as He has in the use of these things? Can you see that He really does have our best interest in mind? Can you see how alcohol and other drugs have caused extreme damage, lasting and far reaching? Can you see how drug and alcohol treatment, that fails to deal with the evil spirits and their chains and landing strips and open doors, usually fails? This is why only Jesus Christ as THE "Higher Power" has been found to be usually the only solution to addiction (as well as every other kind of problem!). Can you see now, why the greek word for witchcraft is "pharmakeia"? Can you see now why God tells us not to associate with, eat with, or ... well let's quote it accurately: I Corinthians 5:11 & 13b, "But now I have written unto you not to keep company, if any man (or woman) that is called a BROTHER, (or sister), be a FORNICATOR, or COVETOUS, or an IDOLATOR, or a RAILER, (one who "bad mouth's" people), or a DRUNKARD, or EXTORTIONER; with such an one no, NOT TO EAT...therefore PUT AWAY FROM AMONG YOURSELVES that wicked person." Again, it's the idea of putting someone under "quarantine" for the best interest of everyone concerned, until repentance and deliverance takes place.

EVEN TO THE THICKNESS OF A SPIDER WEB

I love my dear friends in the Body of Christ so very very deeply! I am so wonderfully grateful for them! I so want to flow with them in the unity of the Holy Spirit that I want nothing to come between us EVEN TO THE THICKNESS OF A COBWEB!!! God says, "Guard earnestly the unity of the Spirit in the bond of peace." Eph.4. and Ps.133:1 "How good and pleasant it is for brethren to dwell together in unity!" and "If we walk in the light as He is in the light, we have fellowship with one another and the blood of Jesus cleanses us from ALL, (not most, but ALL) sin!" I Jn.1:7.

GOD'S ARMY WANTS YOU!!!

One of my favorite passages of Scripture is the second chapter of Joel, at least the first part. (The last half is kind of tuff.) Included there is a beautiful description of the end time army of the Lord of which we can be a part, if we qualify. (See my book, *How TO Rule The World or Seek 1st The Kingdom Of God!)* Anyway, this Army is described as follows, (which means you can't be a part of it unless you "fit the description"). It says, "They don't break rank, nor do they THRUST ONE ANOTHER THROUGH.!" Here, let's quote it from the King James: "...They shall march every one on His ways, and they shall not break their ranks: Neither shall one thrust another; they shall walk every one in His path: and when they fall upon the sword, they shall not be wounded."

ONLY ONE IN STEP

Reminds me of the time I played the big bass drum in the marching band. Nearly everyone in the band determines how fast to march based on the beat of the big base drum, as they couldn't always see the guy in the front with the ball on his stick and who wore the funny looking hat. Anyhow during practice one day, the band director stops the whole band in the middle of the street and comes running back, his face livid with rage. He yelled at me, "John Bohlen, I'll have you know, you're the ONLY ONE IN THIS WHOLE BAND WHO'S OUT OF STEP!" To which I calmly replied, but firmly and so's everyone could hear, "Sir, I'll have you know, I'm the only one in this whole blessed band who is IN step." Everyone laughed, including the director, and we marched on down the street, in step.

SECRET OF UNITY OR "TAUT THAT FLAUT!"

I also played the timpani in the symphony. We also had a flute section with several flute players, sometimes pronounced by high brows as "flautists". Some people in the Lord think that the Body of Christ ought to be run like this: where the third flutist, or flautist, as the case may be, toots his flute based on when and what he, or she sees or hears the second flautist flauting and or tauting, who in turn toots and flauts based on what he, or she hears and/or sees the first flautist flauting and/or tauting or tooting, as the case may be. No. They play in "concert" or in "symphony" or in "harmony" when they are all following the written music while watching the director. We too must never arrive at unity based on compromising the will of God as we see it - but on conformity to the will of God based on the written or living Word of God while watching our heavenly Orchestra Director, the Holy Spirit".

MR. CLEAN

Bible says, "So if, when you are offering your gift at the altar and then remember that your brother has any [grievance] against you, leave your gift at the altar and go," (NOT TO SOMEONE ELSE, but) "first make peace with your brother, and THEN come back and present your gift." Matthew 5:23 & 24. Why do you think that our Lord gave us these instructions? I believe that our 'gift' includes the giving of not only our money but also of our prayers, our praise, even our very life! But will we practice this commandment? or pay heed to these following verses?

"That your prayers be not hindered" I Peter 3, the whole chapter. Here, The Lord says that a poor relationship between a husband and wife will result in their prayers being hindered!

"Don't let the sun go down on your wrath..." Eph.4:26. What a lovely policy for a couple to follow, and for all of us in the Body of Christ!

"Guard earnestly the unity of the faith in the bond of peace..." Eph.4:3 It is something that sometimes has to be worked at!

"Be ye clean that bear the vessels of the Lord..." Isaiah 52:11.

PHOENIX

A number years ago we pioneered and pastored a church in Phoenix, Arizona. All the while I pastored, I determined that I would refuse to preach or prophesy, sing or pray, counsel or minister if I was aware of a wrong relationship either with the Lord or with my wife. As a lovely testimony to God's ability to enable us to keep a right spirit, a right heart, I can't remember withholding even one time of ministry because of this.

But I do remember one time I came pretty close! It happened one Sunday morning while preparing for church. I became aware that something was wrong in my relationship with my wife. I tried everything I knew: pleading, repenting, scolding, questioning - all to no avail. There was a wall between us that I just couldn't seem to break through. So, with about 15 minutes to spare before church was to start, I jumped in the car, drove to the nearest shopping center and quickly purchased for Karen some sweet smellum's skunk water type perfume, some sweet tastums kind of candy, and a pretty sweet-something card, and had these gift wrapped. Then I hurried back to church as the service was beginning and only had time to walk past my wife where she was sitting, and gently lay these gifts in her lap on my way up to the front. When I next turned to look at her, the tears of repentance and forgiveness and restoration and love were streaming down her cheeks. So we got to minister that day as well. Glory be to God! And this is a policy that we still follow, and recommend to others, because God Himself commands it!

REMEMBER: GOD DEMANDS THAT WE ALWAYS MAINTAIN A RIGHT HEART ATTITUDE AND A RIGHT SPIRIT, AT ALL TIMES AND IN EVERYTHING! Furthermore - we have seen how He makes it possible on a practical level.

SUMMARY

Here, we have attempted to describe instances of Kingdom Protocol in matters of unity, criticism, submission, authority-subordinate relationships, etc. We trust that the way has been made more clear in these sometimes complicated matters.

Dear Heavenly Father, Please grant that we will always properly relate to each other at all times, and in everything, and that we will always properly relate to You — in them!!! For Thy Greatest Glory - In Jesus' Name. Amen.

CHAPTER 9 — REVIEW

1. If God asks us to do plan A and the ministries tell us to do plan B, what should we do?

2. Does anyone have a right to "cross" our conscience?

3. Are we absolved from moral responsibility if we are acting in blind submission to another?

4. Do we have a right to voice our leadings if they are contrary to the opinion of those in authority?

5. True or False: "Those in authority are superior to those who the subordinate."

6. What, in your opinion, is the "best" form of government?

7. Complete this thought: "If a person has a sell out price, _____."

8. What is the "worst" form of prostitution?

9. What phrase or thought immediately follows the Scripture which says, "Rebuke not an elder"?

10. Is there such a thing a "righteous" rebellion?

11. Give at least 7 Bible examples of "righteous" rebellion?

12. Has God ever repented?

13. Did Moses ever make it into the Promised Land?

14. Please complete this thought: "We must always be submissive to the Christ, wherever _____ _____ ."

15. "But we must never be submissive to _____
    _____ .

16. When are we to be submissive to those "over" us in the Lord?

17. When Peter, having Christ's best interest in mind, gave Him a human opinion, how did Christ respond?

18. Why do you think Jesus responded as He did?

19. Briefly describe each of the Four "Horses", and what they symbolize.

20. Complete this Bible phrase: "Rebellion is as the sin of _____ ."

21. As in the illustration of Timbuck, can God give the same couple opposite moving directions?

22. Can you pray this prayer: "Lord, if You aren't getting glory from my life, please change me, and if You see that You cannot change me, then please kill me, rather than allow me to bring shame to Your Name!" ?

23. Will you pray that prayer?

24. Suppose you have a problem, a criticism or a disagreement with another in the Body of Christ. Does God or the Bible EVER allow you to go to a third party, before you FIRST go to the person with whom one has a problem?

25. Can you think of any situation or time when repentance would not be appropriate if you get criticized or rebuked?

26. Name between 4 and 7 situations when we are not to associate or eat with others in the Body of Christ.

27. Is God either "religious" or "legalistic", according to the book's definition?

28. Why are we not to associate or eat with so-called brothers or sisters in Christ who are practicing fornication, drunkenness or gossip?.

29. Explain what is meant by "inextricable intermingling."

30. Who is the foundation of the Church?

31. Are we supposed to "take the speck" out of our brother's eye?

Chapter 10 - Outline

DECLARATION OF WAR

I. "Curses On The Enemy"

II. War

III. "Potshots At Important People" or "Roast Preacher"
  A. Kenneth Hagin
  B. David Wilkerson
  C. An Old Friend Named John

IV. How To Tell The Guilty Guys

V. Balaam's Ass

VI. Review

PRACTICAL APPLICATIONS
or
DECLARATION OF WAR
or
BLESSED ARE THE "PEACEMAKERS"

"Curses On The Enemy"

A friend of mine quotes it this way, "Be as wise as a serpent, and as harmless..." (smile).

Another like it, and perhaps more familiar, "Do unto others, before they get a chance to do it to you."

Or still another, "Do good to your brother, (Do him real good)!"

The Bible's Old Testament comes to a solemn close with the word "curse" and the threat of one. (Let the reader beware!) "Behold, I will send you the spirit of Elijah the prophet before the coming of the great and dreadful day of the Lord;" "And He shall turn the heart of the fathers to the children and the heart of the children to their fathers, lest I will come and smite the earth with a curse." Malachi 4:5 & 6.

We once a part of a group of churches that began to do just the opposite, and they have been cursed by the Lord ever since. Then they began to have other problems too, such as immorality, man worship, drunkenness, exclusivity, arrogance, isolationism, cannibalism, unteachableness, any one of which could bring the wrath of God. In fact, the judgement has already begun. When the Christ within us was no longer received, God led us on. Remember when Christ sent out the twelve and the seventy, two by two? He gave them explicit instructions that when their ministry was no longer received that they should go on down the road to where it would be received. We suggest that you do the same, (unless the problem lies with you, in which case maybe you should go anyway. God can dump it on you better when there's no umbrella). Jesus also indicated that the rejectors of His "sent ones" would be severely the losers, and that it would be credited to their account as having been done to Christ. Remember, IT IS ACCREDITED TO OUR ACCOUNT AS HAVING BEEN DONE TO CHRIST, THE WAY WE RELATE TO EVEN THE LEAST OF THOSE WHO ARE DOING THE WILL OF GOD and it becomes accredited to the account of others, as having been done to Christ, the way they relate to us when we are doing the will of God.

When the Lord talks about, "Blessed are the peacemakers", He is not talking about a six-gun! (Though He did say "Sell your cloak and buy a sword." Don't ask me what that means.)

MINISTRIES OF UNITY

God has given to the Church a special task force of ministries that are especially qualified to help bring unity to the Body of Christ, although all of us are called to be peace makers. These ministries are called "foundational ministries". Eph.2:20, "You are built upon the FOUNDATION OF THE APOSTLES AND PROPHETS, Jesus Christ Himself being the Chief Corner Stone!" If, in a average gathering of Christians, (the born-again ones are the only kind there is), you ask the question, "Who is the foundation of the Church?" Less than one out of ten thousand Christians will answer that the apostles and prophets are to be the foundation of the Church!!! No wonder so many churches are built upon the wrong foundation!

Note this Scripture and see who and what we mean: "God has given, (is giving, and will continue to give -Greek arorist tense) some to be apostles, and some as prophets, and some as evangelists and some as pastors and some as teachers...UNTIL WE ALL BECOME ONE in the faith." Ephesians 4:11, & 13a. God's Church has failed to get God's results because we have failed to follow God's formula.

WAR

We invite you to declare war against hatred and disunity in the Body of Christ. But what do we mean by "Declaration of War"? Let me explain. The Bible clearly indicates that we are to keep a right spirit at all times, but it also states that we are to "Be angry, and sin not"! What this means is that we are commissioned to have a white hot righteous anger as a deep motivation, even the zeal and indignation of the Lord Himself against all of the sin that opposes Him and His Kingdom.

Imagine that you are sitting in a restaurant with your family and a bully comes to your table and begins pulling your wife's hair. What would you do? It is clear that if you personally are attacked, that you and I are to "turn the other cheek", and "go the second mile" and "Rejoice, when folks say all manner of evil against us falsely" for the Lord's sake. But notice something! It NEVER states that if I am standing by and a person comes up to my brother or sister, and smites him or her on the one cheek that I must turn MY other. It also does not prohibit me from stepping in between the two parties and act as a peace maker. In fact, I firmly believe that if my brother or sister is being brutalized, murdered, mobbed, mugged, maimed, molested, dismembered or massacred in our presence that we must NOT stand weakly meekly sweetly by and allow it to continue. The thought of this is unthinkable and wrong in the eyes of God and should be wrong in ours! But there have been too many soft-bellied-weak-kneed sissies in the body of Christ that have allowed this kind of thing to happen too many times! If it was not my fault that someone hit my brother or sister the first time, it sure as heaven is true that I am guilty if a second blow was landed!!! For if I stand by and allow my sister or brother to be brutalized in my presence, then I am as guilty as was Saul at the stoning of Stephen; and so are you!

The Scriptures say that "If your brother offends you, GO TO HIM"! (Matt.18:5), and "Rebuke not an elder but GO TO HIM"! (I Tim.5:1). But no place in the Scriptures does it ever say that we are to first go to someone else about him. Therefore, I have personally declared a holy war against the unbridled cannibalization of my sister or brother in my presence. I invite you to do the same.

"POTSHOTS AT IMPORTANT PEOPLE"
or
"ROAST PREACHER FOR SUNDAY DINNER"

Have you ever heard the expression "Having Roast Preacher for Sunday Dinner"? As we said in another place, many parents gossip and back bite their pastor at Sunday's dinner in front of their children, and then wonder why their children have no respect for the people and things of God when they get older. (Not to excuse disrespect.) Have you seen that the basis for much criticism is jealousy?

KENNETH HAGIN

Let me give you an example: I was in a church situation one Lord's Day when the pastor and others began making some snide negative, sarcastic remarks about Kenneth Hagin. So I raised my hand and gently asked the question, "How many of you here, that have a disagreement with Brother Hagin, have ever tried to call him, or write him or send him a tape or otherwise contact him, about your criticism?"

As you might expect, NOT ONE OF THEM HAD!!! So I quietly explained that first of all the Scriptures make it quite plain that we have absolutely no right to stab or bite our brother's back until we have first gone to him with the problem. God and His Bible say, "Go to him!" NOT "Go to some busy body else and back bite about him." (Matt.18:15; I Tim.5:1).

I then went on to explain to the group how that one time Brother Hagin had done something that offended me, that I disagreed with and that I didn't like. But rather than to grump and groan and chicken around behind to bite his back, I sent him a letter. Now Brother Hagin must get a lot of letters from a lot of people, and furthermore, he doesn't know me from Adam last, so I could hardly expect a reply, but a short while later, along came a personal letter from Brother Kenneth Hagin. In his letter to me, he had taken the time to answer, and in it, he humbled himself and apologized to me and asked me to forgive him. I had refused to gossip against him in the first place and I was proud of him in the second place and publicly applaud his humility in the third place. Can you agree?

Now in the above paragraph, I used the phrase "chicken around behind to bite his back". On the Iowa farm we raised chickens. When one would develop a problem with a sore, the other chickens would pick 'n peck on it until they had literally pick-pecked that poor chicken to death! That's why I say that it's really really chicken to back bite on our brother (or sister) unless first we have gone to them in

love. I say it's "chicken"! God says it is "SIN"!
Remember when we said earlier that you don't need
to put a lid on a bucket of crabs, because when one of
them starts to make a little progress toward freedom,
the rest of the crabs pull him (or her) down. I believe
we have some "crabs" in the Body of Christ. Are you
one of them?

DAVID WILKERSON

I was at a meeting where David Wilkerson spoke at
the Jesus' People Church in 1982 where I thought he
was too critical. But a short time later came his
newsletter where he was humbling himself to the
body of Christ at large and asking for rebukes,
corrections, criticisms and feedback from any and all
who would write to him, and he promised to earnestly
pray about what was sent. Then, in his next letter, he
told about how God had really spoken to him through
these letters and that he had deeply repented of many
things on his face before God, and further, was asking
for the prayers and forgiveness of everyone. As near
as I can tell, that repentance has been real, and lasting.
Of course he has the mantle of a modern day prophet
of God who is calling the people to repentance; but,
like the old time prophets of God, he is learning to
identify himself with the sins of the people as one of
them, being one with them, interceding for them.
Amen! Besides, Prophets are to be loving and sweet.

SANCTIFIED CRITICISM

Would you believe that there is a place for criticism
in the body of Christ and the Kingdom of God? There
is!

221

Bible says, "Rebuke not an elder but GO TO HIM, (NOT SOMEONE ELSE!) and plead with him as a son to a father"! I Tim.5:1. Some people think that the sentence, the verse, the chapter, the book & the Bible closes right after the phrase, "Rebuke not an elder...." I believe that in the original text there was not even a comma!

Bible says that after we have removed the beam or log out of our own eye, that THEN we are to GO TO OUR BROTHER, (NOT SOMEBODY ELSE!) and remove the lint or the splinter out of our brother's (or sister's) eye. Matthew 7:1-5 & Lk.6:42.

OTHER MINISTRIES — A DEEP NEED

An oft' recurring problem pattern in the body of Christ seems to run something like this: A man or woman attains a place of influence in a ministry. At first, in the early days, they tend to be more teachable, more approachable, more easily intreatable. I remember when I was about twenty years old, I was putting in a concrete driveway for a minister who had retired. I remember asking him this question, "Sir," I said, "If you were to give to me, a young man just starting out in the ministry, any one piece of advice, what would it be?" We had been visiting along while I was working. After thinking about my question a few moments, he said quietly, to this effect, "My young friend, if I were to give you one piece of advice, it would be this, 'ALWAYS REMAIN AS TEACHABLE AS YOU ARE RIGHT NOW!' " (I asked our friend evangelist-prophet Leonard Ravenhill one time in our home the same question. He said, "Always, above all things—be a worshipper!") But as to this thing of being teachable or approachable, the problem is that when a ministry becomes "successful" or "influential" or "widely known and respected" or gets a "large following" or a "large budget" with a "large staff" that they tend to start believing their own publicity and, like many "successful" people begin developing a "god complex"! For example, many lawyers and doctors, social workers, policeman and other ministries forget that they are the "servants of the people" and get to thinking that the people are their servants, instead. How sad!

A FRIEND NAMED JOHN

Once upon a time, I had a friend named John, for example, who started out beautifully, and years ago wonderfully influenced men like Larry Christiansen, Bob Mumford, Jack Winter and Ted Hegre. The group of over 100 flourishing churches became hideously cultic after having been beautiful before God! They got off track for some of the following reasons: 1) They never really had a revelation of "The King's Greatest Secret"! 2) Consequently, they didn't have faith for constant victory in the first place, nor did they genuinely repent, but excused themselves in the second place, because they felt that they "couldn't help themselves" for "after all, they were only human". 3) This Augustinian dualism, Greek manicheist mentality resulted in a "greasy grace" and "sloppy agape" pendulum swing away from legalism

223

and a fear of being religious (as opposed to being spiritual). People were accused of being religious or legalistic if they didn't drink, etc. 4) This resulted in problems of immorality and drunkenness, profanity and irreverence. In their fear of being religious, they became irreligious and sacrilegious. 5) They became exclusivistic, thinking that they had a corner on God, and that others in the Body of Christ were wrong, so this group isolated themselves against flowing with what God was doing in the Body of Christ at large. 6) They placed too much emphasis on one man, and the words he spoke, and thus got off into "man-worship". They became overly submissive to man and ministry, and failed to be submissive to God.

But couldn't all this have been avoided? Of course! If only the leadership could have been humble and teachable!

This leader got into desperate straights spiritually and other ways largely because he became increasingly unreceptive to wise counsel from "subordinate" channels of the Lord's Word. God would raise up Nathan-prophet-like ministries to be able to say "Thou art the man!" In fact, there is a long list of ministries that through the years tried to give him corrective suggestions, but who were systematically discredited, rejected, isolated, restricted, sued, lied about, and prayed against, (we have heard that he even had a prayer-"hit" list) cannibalistically by means of psychic intimidation and "Christian" witchcraft! Now, we have heard that he died slowly from cancer. Like David, we say, "How are the

224

mighty fallen!" and "There, but for the grace of God, go I." Instead of morbidly wondering who he was, please note this fact. God has obligated himself by His own nature and promise to "resist the proud". (James 4:6 & I Peter 5:5) We obligate God to resist us when we become unteachable and arrogant. There are many, many ministries in the body of Christ today who are similarly unteachable! Would you like to know who they are?

HOW TO TELL THE GUILTY GUYS

All one has to do in order to tell if a ministry is uncorrectable is—-CORRECT HIM!!! Then watch his reaction. Don't rebuke him, but "GO TO HIM, AND PLEAD WITH HIM AS A SON TO A FATHER" Does he (or she) stay sweet in their spirit? Bible says, "Correct a wise man and he will love you."! Proverbs 9:8. If your spiritual leader will not listen to wise counsel from the Christ through a subordinate channel, then we recommend that prayer be made that the leadership become teachable, and if the leadership still refuses to be teachable, approachable, etc. then we respectfully recommend that you ask the Lord to give you shepherds after His own heart. The quickest way to open up the door to deception from the enemy is to be unteachable or uncorrectable in your spirit or to follow someone else who is unteachable or uncorrectable. We teach the dear ones that "ONE MUST KEEP A RIGHT SPIRIT EVEN IF THE WRONG PERSON COMES TO HIM AT THE WRONG TIME WITH A

WRONG SPIRIT, SHARING WRONG INFOR-
MATION IN A WRONG MANNER, AND EVEN
REACH INTO GOD TO BENEFIT FROM THE
EXPERIENCE!!!"

I remember back in the olden days at Bible school at Bethany Fellowship. It was the first time I ever "prophesied". I was so timid, (believe it or not)! It took a long time to work up enough courage to "do a prophecy". Finally, I took a breath and "did a prophecy"! Oh, it was short, and probably wasn't much, but it was my "loaves and fishes" sure enough, and afterwards, I felt so glad that I had "obeyed the Lord". But guess what? Sure enough, after the meeting, an upperclass student took me aside out in the hallway and with solemn look and somber tone, said something like this: "John, I just wanted you to know that your prophecy was of the "flesh" and there was an awful lot of John Bowlunball (of course there was!) in that prophecy you did, an' uh a person needs to be mighty careful when he does a prophecy, 'cause you could git off track 'n things like that." I smiled at him and said, "Thank you David," and immediately I sought a place of prayer where I could talk things over with the Lord. I explained the situation to the Lord, (as if He wasn't up-to-date on the situation). Then it seemed like the Lord said to me, "Son, you're doing just fine! Be encouraged! Keep on keeping on! I love you and I will continue to lead you by My Spirit." But, if I had become defensive, or withdrawn, or fearful, or self pitying, I would have missed the reassuring voice of the Lord to me. Instead, I actually ended up being strengthened in the thing about which I had received criticism!!!

BALAAM'S ASS

Remember in Numbers 22 of the Bible how God spoke to the prophet Balaam, through his donkey?!. Isaiah 11:6 says, "A little child shall lead them." Ephesians 5:21 starts out the section on husbands and wives by saying that they are to be submissive TO EACH OTHER in the fear of God, which means to me that there are times when the husband will be submissive to his wife! "Sarah called Abraham 'lord'." But do you fellows remember when God told Abraham, "Do as she says!" or did you guys forget about that one? Genesis 21:12.

Sometimes God will speak to you through a woman, a child a donkey, or perhaps even a man. And when He does speak, then we had better listen, and we had better hear, and we had better obey!!! God grant all of us that we always have a godly fear and trembling, lest we fail to hear or rightly relate to the Christ in the very least of the dear ones who are doing the will of God. God grant that we rightly relate to the Christ WHEREVER He is found, and THROUGH WHOM EVER HE SPEAKS!!! In Jesus' Holy Name. AMEN!

Dear Heavenly Father, please grent I always rightly relate to You, wherever You are found and through whomever You chose to speak. Please grant that we never wrongly relate to You, by wrongly relating to the least of these who do Your will. In Jesus Name, Amen.

CHAPTER 10 — REVIEW

1. What curse does the Old Testament close with?
2. If people refuse to accept the ministry of Christ through you, what should you do?
3. Complete this Kingdom Principle: IT IS ACCREDITED TO OUR ACCOUNT AS HAVING BEEN DONE TO CHRIST.
4. What do we mean "declare holy war" against cannibalism?
5. What do chickens do when one of their fellow members have a problem sore?
6. What is meant by a "god complex"?
7. What is one of the best ways to find out if a person is correctable?
8. If your spiritual leader persists in his unteach-ableness, what should you do?
9. Use the word "wrong" at least 5 times in completing the Kingdom Principle: "One must keep a right spirit, at all times, even if _____ _____ .
10. What Scripture precedes the verse in Ephesians 5 which tells the wife to be submissive to the husband as to the Lord?
11. Complete this thought: "God grant that we always be submissive to and rightly relate to the Christ, wherever _____ _____ .

Chapter 11 — Outline
CULTS, THE OCCULT, & YOUR CULT

I. Man Worship & Salem Witches

II. Report From Christianity Today.

III. Application.

IV. Blaspheming the Holy Spirit — the Unforgiveable Sin!

V. Call For Consistency.

CHAPTER 11

CULTS, OCCULTS, and YOUR CULT!

Remember hearing about the Salem, Massachusetts witch trials and hangings? I heard that the real truth is that the real witches were so clever and powerful that they rigged things to happen in such a way that not one witch ended up being killed, but that only innocent people were framed, falsely accused and executed. According to the story, there were warlocks and witches actually doing the trying, judging and executing! Do you realize that often the same thing happens today in our zeal to see cults and cult members convicted? Let me explain.

One of the best definitions I ever heard, of the word "cult", is: "Anybody that believes different than me!" But to be perfectly serious, I recommend to you that you look up the word "cult" in your favorite dictionary! You'll probably find out that YOU belong to one!!! Most dictionaries give as their main definition, "A system of religious beliefs and practices"!!!, and most dictionaries have nothing negative in their definitions!

Perhaps you know someone who would say, "Any fool knows what a cult is!" To which I reply, " 'Tis all too true, most fools think they do!" You see, they crucified Christ, because they thought that He was cultic; and they crucified and killed Christians, because they thought that these Christians were heretics and cultic.

Please understand, that I understand, that the word "occult", and cult as they are used today have some negative connotations, but I have also looked in two major dictionaries, and could find no negative inferences in the definition of the word "occult".

Now I understand, (or at least I think I do) the words as they are commonly used by most Christians. Most Christians define a "cult" as being, "some body who believes different from me"!!!

Dear Lord, please grant that we have more love for these who are in error. If we did Lord, couldn't we win them out of their "cults" more often than we do??! Help us here, too, to hate the sin, but to always love the sinner, and to be so humble in our awful sense of rightness, that we will ALWAYS "COUNT ALL OTHERS AS BETTER THAN OURSELVES"!!! (PH.2:3) Father, please grant that, as we seek to restore them, that we shall seek to do so "in a spirit of meekness, considering ourselves, lest we also be tempted." (Gal.6:1) In Jesus' Name, Amen.

CULT VS. NON-CULT

I believe that a person or a group is cultic to the extent that we or they FAIL to meet the following guidelines:

1. We must believe that "THE FIRST AND GREAT COMMANDMENT" is: "THOU SHALT LOVE THE LORD THY GOD WITH ALL THY HEART, AND WITH ALL THY SOUL, AND WITH ALL THY MIND"!!! Jesus said this in Matthew 22. He said, "THIS IS THE FIRST AND GREATEST COMMANDMENT"! Then Jesus said, "AND THE SECOND IS LIKE UNTO IT"!

2. We must believe that "ABOVE ALL THINGS, WE MUST LOVE EACH OTHER FERVENTLY, FROM A PURE HEART!" and Love each other as much as we do ourselves - (Is this too strong? Wow!!! Do you suppose that this what God meant when He commanded, "Love your neighbor as yourself"??? I Peter 1:22; 4:8; Matthew 22).

3. We must believe that the Bible is (in the original), the inspired, infallible, trust-in-able, build-your-life-on-able, let-your-weight-down-on-able Word of God.

4. We must believe that Jesus Christ is God!!!

5. We must believe in Christ's resurrection from the dead.

6. We must believe in the resurrection of all mankind to God's judgement of ever-lasting life or ever-lasting hell.

7. We must believe in the virgin birth of Christ.

8. We must believe that it is ABSOLUTELY NECESSARY to be "born-again" by specifically inviting Jesus Christ to reign within as one's personal Lord and Saviour.

9.   We must believe that it is necessary to do the will of God if we expect to "inherit the Kingdom of God" (Mat. 7:21)! If you have any questions about this one, please read the New Testament again, with an open heart.

10.   We must believe that Father, Son and Holy Ghost must be our ONLY Lord and Master! We must NOT be "man worshippers", or have respect for a person or people OVER our respect for God!!!

"MAN WORSHIP"

This of course means that we MUST NOT HAVE AN IDOL WORSHIPPING OR AN idolatrous over-appreciation for the pope, Sun or Moon, Jim Jones, Mary Baker Eddy, Mary White, Mary - the mother of Christ - or any other Mary, Joseph, (St or Smith), your church founder, leader, pastor, radio preacher, or TV evangelist !!! We must not be "exclusivistic" to the point of thinking "our group or church or church demonization is the only thing, an' if you ain't in our church, then you ain't any thing..." Jesus said that He, Jesus Christ the Creator King of Every thing, is "THE Way, THE Truth and THE Life and no one, (that means NO BODY) COMES UNTO THE FATHER EXCEPT THROUGH HIM." The Bible also says that, "There is only one God, and one Mediator between God and men, the Man, Christ Jesus." I Tim.2:5. This means that the leader of your group or any other group is NOT ANOTHER MEDIATOR between you and God. God is jealous over you in this

233

regard and He will not share His Glory or His Lordship with ANY other.

I once heard a man of God they called "John" say to his group, "The day we think we've got a corner on God, that's the day we've lost it!" But the day DID come for them when they thought that they had a "corner on God" and they DID lose it, and it WAS a sad day. That day can come for you and me too, unless you and I stay very, VERY humble and tender before the Lord God!

OTHER "SALVATION" VERSES

The Apostle Paul says, "But though we, or an angel from heaven, preach any other gospel unto you than that which we have preached unto you, let him be accursed." (Galatians 1:8) But please notice two things about the Apostle Paul. (#1) Just a few verses later, in chapter 2, verse 11: "But when Peter was come to Antioch, I withstood him to his face, because he was to be blamed." And we must withstand each other also, if we do what Peter did when he was contributing to separation and divisions in the body of Christ!!! A few verses later, in 5:15, Paul says, "But if ye BITE and DEVOUR one another, TAKE HEED that ye be not CONSUMED one of another". He then goes on to mention "hatred, variance (disagreement, dissension, dispute,) emulations, (jealous rivalry, man worship,) wrath, strife, seditions, (incitement of, resistance to, or insurrection against God's delegated authority), heresies, envyings...and such like: of the which I tell you before, as I have also told you in time past, that they which do such things shall NOT INHERIT THE KINGDOM OF GOD"!!!

And although Paul mentions heresy here, please notice the second thing. Paul told Felix the governor that he, Paul, was now part of a group of people who were known as HERETICS! "But this I confess unto thee, that after the way which THEY CALL HERESY, so worship I the God of my fathers..."! Acts 24.

Think about this! Someone has said that THE THING GOD DOES IN ONE GENERATION ALMOST ALWAYS PERSECUTES THE THING GOD DOES IN THE FOLLOWING GENERATION.

APPLICATION

There is too much name calling, division, petty silliness, back-biting, gossip, and discord in the body of Christ, and God is angry about it. (Prov.6:16-20). Let me give you some examples: There are those in the Minneapolis and St Paul area, and in the body of Christ at large who will not fellowship or flow with or accept certain others because of petty disagreements over and about things like the following: Baptism, the Baptism with (or is it "by", or "of", or "in", oh yeah, "in") the Holy Spirit, and its "evidence", (the evidence is LOVE!), and the "rupture" (pronounced rapture, although some pronounce it "the grand snatch"!), and survival, and mortal majority, and "faith teaching" (what's the alternative, "unbelief" teaching?), and the manifestation of the sons of God, (everybody manifests something!), and charismatics, (aren't they nice?) and movies, (aren't they awful), etc., etc., etc., ad nauseam. I have an apostle friend that the Lord has appeared to, and spoken to, many times. He was called a false prophet by someone, simply because he heard the man of God say something that he, the critic, had not heard before!!! This critic mentioned my friend to another critic, (who had a sour spirit). The sour spirit, (a good Christian fellow who works in a Christian book store) then may have committed the unpardonable sin of blaspheming the Holy Spirit, when he turned around and said that my apostle friend was of the devil. Some folks think they know all there is to know about God! (They know all they are going to - until they know they don't!)

BLASPHEMING THE HOLY SPIRIT

In Matthew 12:31, Jesus says that "blasphemy against the Holy Spirit shall NOT be forgiven", and the context tells us clearly that Jesus spoke this as a direct response to folks who said that what Jesus did was of the devil!!! And yet many times I have heard good Christians say this to other good Christians about other good Christians. BLASPHEMING THE HOLY SPIRIT IS ATTRIBUTING TO SATAN THAT WHICH IS OF GOD! Blaspheming the Holy Spirit is simply saying that something or someone is of the devil, that may well be of God!!! And Jesus said that this sin is NEVER forgivable, either in this age OR in the ages to come! If you have never committed this sin, we respectfully recommend that you never do! And if you think you may have committed this sin, we suggest that you get and read our book entitled, *How to Rule the World, or, Seek first the Kingdom of God,* Write to: Great Commission Ministries, P.O. 7123, Minneapolis, Mn., 55407. (We recommend it anyway). We suggest that if you think you may have sinned it all away, that you repent anyway, and invite Jesus into your heart and live your life 100% for Him anyway and praise and worship Him anyway at all times and in every circumstance, no matter what, any way and every way!!! Amen.

LET'S BE CONSISTENT

We mentioned earlier about being impaled on your yardstick, or "Meted by your measure" (Mat.7:2; Mk.4:24; Lk.6:28). We know of groups that are accused of being a "cult", even though the so called "cult" believes in the virgin birth, the deity of Christ, the Lordship of Christ, the validity of the Scriptures, the blood of Jesus, the bodily resurrection, salvation by accepting Jesus as Saviour and Lord into their hearts. They may be labeled a "cult" for placing too much emphasis on one doctrine, or they may have too much respect for a particular man or woman, or because the group is too exclusive, (we shouldn't be). But, at the same time we FAIL to apply this same yardstick to countless religious leaders and pastors of Methodist, and Episcopalian, and Lutheran, and Baptist, and Congregational, and Presbyterian, and other churches IF or WHEN THEY DON'T BELIEVE IN the deity of Christ, or salvation by inviting Christ in as Lord and Saviour so we can be born again, or DON'T believe in the Validity of the Scriptures, or the atoning merit and power of the blood of Jesus Christ, or Christ's resurrection or return but who at the same time are ALSO exclusive, or lopsided, or place too much emphasis on a man or woman, (Pope or Mary included). How terribly inconsistent!

Christianity Today, in a news summary from October 13, 1967, gave a report from a survey taken by sociologist Jeffrey Hadden, who received 7,441 questionnaires from a cross section of ministers from major denominations, indicating that vast percentages of main-line denominations do NOT BELIEVE in these all important doctrines. If you are going to name call and cult call, then let's apply the same yard stick to all — to the denominations too. Then you tell me who is the cult!!!

Just because a denomination, group or church has existed for x amount of years has absolutely nothing to do with its favor in God's eyes. All through history, God has had for Himself a precious remnant of dear ones who walk with Him uncompromisingly, and with total love and dedication. And usually, these people, where ever they have been, or what ever they have been called, have been the harried, harassed, persecuted, ill thought of minority. As we said before, that which was blessed of God in one generation, often ended up persecuting that which God was blessing in the next. Let's not even hold the coats of these persecutors.

CHAPTER 11 — REVIEW

1. How does this author define the word "cult"?

2. Give a dictionary definition of the word "cult".

3. Give your definition of the word "cult".

4. What is absolutely necessary before we can win others from their wrong doctrine or group?

5. What does Galatians 5:15 say?

6. Make a list of at least 17 things that will keep folks out of God's Kingdom if they fail to repent. (You may look these up.) Mat.7:21; Gal.5:19-21; I Cor.6:9.10

7. According to Acts 24, was Paul, after his conversion, part of a group known as heretics, or known for their heresy?

8. Would YOU be willing to belong to such a group?

9. Define the meaning of the phrase, "Blaspheming the Holy Spirit".

10. What do we mean, "Impaled On Your Yardstick"?

11. Please give a guess at how many hours it would take to read through the entire Bible, at pulpit reading speed, without skipping any parts.

12. Have you ever read the Bible through in this manner?

CHAPTER 12 — OUTLINE

TUFF LUV

I. Tuff Luv
II. Poor Little Suzie
III. Inextricable Intermingling
IV. 2 (or) 3 Pionts of View
V. Danger Quarantine
VI. God Ain't Religious
VII. Drugs and Their Effect
VIII. The Positive Side
IX. Restoration and Healing
X. Sympathy
XI. Minister to Me on My Terms
XII. Spiritual Prostitution
XIII. Infant Extortion
XIV. Phoney Phoning
XV. You Ain't Bled Yet!

12

TUFF LUV
&
KINGDOM QUARANTINE!!!
SCRIPTURAL DISCIPLINE
or
SPIRITUAL QUARANTINE

What should a pastor or church do if a member continues to commit adultery, gossip, or drunkenness, and refuses to repent or be delivered from it?

We refuse to give our own opinion or answer to this question! Instead, we turn to the Bible to get God's answer. What does the Bible, the Word of God, say in this situation? Does God ever tell the leaders or the Church to practice spiritual "quarantine"?

The Webster's Dictionary defines quarantine as: "...any isolation imposed to keep contagious diseases, etc. from spreading." or "a place for such isolation."

Ministers of the Gospel frequently have their greatest difficulties and problems over the matter of spiritual discipline. But some of their greatest problems would be solved if they would practice God's instructions for Scriptural or Spiritual "Quarantine".

Here are only a few Scriptures that deal with the subject:

Matthew 10:12-15 (Shake the dust)

Matthew 18:15-18 (Go, then 2-3, then the body, then...)

Matthew 21:12 & Mark 11:15 (Jesus & the money changers)

Luke 17:3 ("If your brother offends you, rebuke him.")

John 20:23 (One's sins are retained if you retain them.)

Acts 5:1-14 (Ananias & Sapphira)

Acts 8:5-24 (Simon the sorcerer)

Acts 13:6-13 (Bar-Jesus the false prophet)

I Corinthians 5, (Whole chapter)

I Corinthians 6, esp. verses 9,10

Galatians 1:6-12

Galatians 5:14-6:1

I Timothy 5:1,20; I Timothy 6:3-6

II Timothy 3

Titus 1:10-13; Titus 3:10

II John 1:9-11

Jude

Revelation 11:3-13

POOR LITTLE SUZIE

Would you think it unkind of parents of a pretty little girl named Suzie to put her in a room by herself, away from the rest of the children, and for them not to allow the rest of the children to play with her? Oh, I forgot to mention that dear little Suzie has come down with a hideously contaminating disease that the others are sure to catch if they have unquarantined contact with her! Some uninformed onlooker might sympathetically conclude that the parents are being very very mean and cruel to isolate poor little Suzie this way.

INEXTRICABLE INTERMINGLING

Some years ago, while ministering at a church, a young man came up and asked, "Could you break my bonds?" I said, "What do you mean?" He said, "Y'know, my physical bonds." He said, "Well, me and my girl friend, we been sorta like messin' around y'know." I said, "You mean you and she have been having intercourse?" He said, "Yeah, I mean, right, and now I'd like for you to break my bonds." I thought for a minute, and then replied, "I'll tell you what. Bring me a half a glass of water, and a half glass of milk. If you can pour them together and then separate them back to their original unmixed condition, I'll 'break your bonds' " (I wanted him to realize the seriousness of his sin.).

2 (or) 3 POINTS OF VIEW

We talked briefly about this in chapter 9, but at this point, we want to tie this in with the idea of Scriptural Quarantine. The playboy says this about the casualness of sex, "It's like shaking hands. That's all there is to it," Playboy says, "afterwards, each goes their separate way, and that's it." And the attitude of the one committing adultery is similar, "Such is the way of an adulterous woman; she eateth, and wipeth

244

her mouth, and saith, I have done no wickedness." Proverbs 30:20.

But GOD'S POINT OF VIEW IS WHAT COUNTS, no matter how far-fetched it seemes to be, and as you might expect, it is different from the playboy or the mouth wiping prostitute. God says that when people have sexual intercourse, they become totally inextricably intermingled, body, soul and spirit, as when one pours two containers of liquid together in such a way that one can never unmix them, (inextricable intermingling).

It is our understanding that the Hebrew word for "rib" can also be equally translated "side". (See the Amplified Bible). With this in mind, consider the following selection from Genesis 2. "But for Adam there was not found an help meet for him. And the Lord God caused a deep sleep to fall upon Adam, and he slept: and He took one of his ribs (or sides), and closed up the flesh instead thereof; and the rib (or side), which the Lord God had taken from man, made He a woman, and brought her unto the man. And Adam said, 'This is now bone of my bones, and flesh of my flesh: she shall be called Woman, because she was taken out of man.' Therefore shall a man leave his father and his mother, and shall cleave unto his wife: and they shall be one flesh (or nature). And they were both naked, the man and his wife, and were not ashamed." (verses 20b-25).

We have a theory, that we of course don't teach as fact, but as a possibility. There is the possibility that the original Adam that God created was so perfect, that Adam had the ability to reproduce without the need for an outside entity, that is being asexually reproductive, but that there was a problem with loneliness, being able to fellowship only with himself, so God put Adam to sleep and took out of him his "female side", closed up his side and made a new creation called a woman, giving her a distinct body, personality, mind and soul. (Please don't scold me for having a theory, don't feel threatened. I'm not saying this is a fact.) But this next part is not theory; it is a fact that when they came together again sexually that they became totally one, once again: body, soul, and spirit!

The Apostle Paul says something interesting here, (doesn't he always). *"Now the body is not for fornication, but for the Lord; and the Lord for the body. Know ye not that your bodies are the members of Christ? Shall I then take the members of Christ, and make them the members of an harlot? God forbid. What? Know ye not that he which is joined to a harlot is ONE BODY? 'For two', saith He, 'shall be one flesh (or nature).' But he that is joined unto the Lord is one spirit. Flee fornication. Every sin that a man doeth is without the body; but he that committeth fornication sinneth against his own body. What? Know ye not that your body is the temple of the Holy Ghost which is in you, which ye have of God, and ye are not your own? For ye are bought with a price: therefore glorify God in your body, and in your spirit, which are God's." I Cor.6:13b,14-20.*

What we are talking about now is fact, not theory. God is saying here that sexual intercourse is like taking a glass of water and a glass of milk, or whatever, and pouring the two back and forth until they become totally blended, or inextribly intermingled. It's not like "wiping your mouth", and it definitely ain't like shaking hands or clinking glasses! Can you see some of the implications here?

For example, a young virgin who is young, beautiful and innocent could be compared with a beautiful crystal chalice with pure water. But she commits fornication, that is, she has intercourse sexually with someone she is not married to. Let's say that the fellow involved is a playboy whoremonger. At the time of this particular intercourse, a terrifying and hideous thing takes place that causes a total and inextricable intermingling of their bodies, souls, personalities, spirits. It would be like inextricably intermingling a glass of water with a cess pool of urine, coffee, slime, vomit, milk, or blood. Can you see why God is against your having sex with anything other than your spouse?

And if he or she commits adultery or fornication with someone else, the inextricable mix simply gets passed along. Could this phenomenon be a partial explanation why there is so much suicide, mental anguish, schizophrenia, split, dual and multiple personality problems among young high school and college men and women, and others???

But there is a solution to the problem!!! Jesus Christ the Lord of The Universe came to earth to suffer the penalty and punishment for OUR sin, so as to provide for our total cleansing, purification, forgiveness, deliverance, restoration, and renewal! He did this by dying on the cross and "taking the rap" for us! But this forgiveness is not ours UNLESS we accept it and appropriate it for ourselves. And we do this by simply opening the door of our lives wide to God and personally inviting Jesus Christ the Creator King of All the Universe to come in like He promises to do in Revelation 3:20. He says, "Look, I'm standing at the door of your life, and I'm knocking. If you will open the door of your life wide to Me and invite Me to come in to take over completely, I will!!!!!!!" But when you invite God to come in to your life, Jesus is not interested in coming in as your guest or as a roomer. He wants to come in as your Lord and Master and God. And when He comes in, He makes you perfectly new, and alive, and vibrant and clean and virginal and forgiven. (I Jn.1:9). A beautiful crystal clear chalice of the purest most wonderful water of life overflowing!!! That's what you become!!!

But to complicate the problem still more, suppose the girl mentioned above, comes to the Lord Jesus Christ, becomes one nature with God, is made crystal clear and pure, reads her Bible, walks with God, sings in the choir and then gets seduced by whoremonger playboy? If she allows herself to have sex with this guy, it would be like forcing Christ Jesus her Life, to be raped!!! Hold on here. Look at this Scripture!: "Shall I then take the members of CHRIST and unite them with a prostitute? NEVER!!!" (I Corinthians 6:15, NIV).

248

DANGER — QUARANTINE ! ! !

The contamination becomes so hideously-terrifyingly-nauseatingly critical, that the Apostle Paul says that if you know of a brother or sister in the Church Body of Christ that is a PRACTICING adulterer or fornicator, that is, any one who is having sex with what they are not married to, that we are: #1. NOT EVEN to be WITH that person, or to fellowship or #2. eat with or #3. worship with such a person but that we are to #4. set such a person out side the Church until there is a witness of full and complete turning away from that hideous kind of sinning!. That person will not only have to repent and turn away from the sin but must also have a deliverance imparted to them in a miracle greater than the miraculous separation of two inextricably inter-mingled cups of liquid!!! The Lord says this in I Corinthians, chapters 5 and 6, and specifically 5:11b & d, "You are NOT TO ASSOCIATE WITH any person who is known as a brother and yet is immoral...or a railer or a drunkard...with such a person you must NOT BREAK BREAD." And verse 13b, "Therefore, put away from among yourselves those wicked persons." The Lord makes it very clear here that He is talking about "Christians", and not unbelievers.

GOD AIN'T RELIGIOUS OR LEGALISTICALLY MEAN

We'll talk more about legalism, but can you see the love of God in these things? God here is not just giving us a bunch of "no-no's" just to be mean. He wants for His people to be healthy, clean and uncontaminated, crystal clear, white and pure. God really does have our best interest in mind! His command is that we not associate with a so-called brother or sister in Christ who is involved in fornication or drunkenness, etc. He commands this so that we do not become hideously contaminated with the "typhoid Mary" kind of contamination that one becomes contaminated with when: they have sex with what they are not married to, or in coming under the influence of alcohol or other drugs or if they have a "railing" or critical spirit, etc.

DRUGS AND THEIR EFFECT ON
THE HUMAN SPIRIT

As we said before, the Greek word for witchcraft in the Bible is "pharmakia", from which we get our words like pharmacy, pharmacist, pharmaceutical, etc. The worship of satan, devils and witchcraft has almost always been accompanied by the use of drugs. And the reason drugs are used, is their effect on the human spirit. When one ingests drugs, there takes place a disintegration of the natural protective cover or outer protective layer of the human soul that allows free access to that person's inner being for the negative spirit realm, thus allowing access to oppression, obsession and possession by demons and evil spirits. The disintegration of that protective covering is similar to the effect of hot water poured on a thin sheet of ice or wax, or acid being poured on a thin sheet of metal. We are told that the real problem in a burn accident is not so much the burn itself, but that the burn destroys the natural protective layer of the skin, and thus allows access for the free invasion of germs and contamination.

Sometimes the "pink elephants", goblins and monsters that had been considered hallucinations have actually been very real and factual things that have not been present or visible before the ingestion of the drug(s). The bar scene from "Star Wars" pictured a room, full of monsters and awful looking creatures. It was probably a pretty good description of the way many bars actually look, if one could "see" in the spirit realm!

If a so called "Christian" takes these drugs, a terrifying thing takes place because Christ is living within, and the door is thrown open for evil spirits to enter or to negatively affect. And because of our unity in the body of Christ, we are easily blessed, or can be negatively affected by, that which exists in our brother or sister in Christ. God doesn't want His dear children to be contaminated by "typhoid disease contaminators", or "trouble-making negative spiritual hitchhikers", and thus He gives instructions for our immunity by putting the source and carrier of contamination INTO ISOLATION UNDER QUARANTINE, until the problem is solved. Can you see the incredible implications of this? Now, some few may theologically argue that "Christians cannot be possessed by evil spirits", but to be perfectly pragmatically practical, devils live where they live

252

and your blessed doctrine won't make any difference to them, except to let them keep on doing their damndest, undercover. Another argument is that, whereas the Lord may be inhabiting a person's spirit, that the evil spirits may be oppressing, obsessing, or possessing a person's mind, soul, heart or body. These evil spirits MUST GO when there is total repentance (complete once for all turning away from all sin), and prayer of deliverance by those in the Body of Christ who have authority from God, who with the word of authority in Jesus' Name cast them out with a word. (Here we recommend the book by Bill Barr from Oconto Ministries entitled "Counselling With Confidence"). We also recommend our book, *The Sexual Ministry,* for married's.

THE POSITIVE SIDE — SYNERGISM

But so much for the unpleasant aspects. God really has some beautiful things in mind in commanding us to sexual purity! The Bible talks about the synergistically positive effect two people (who are one in Christ-in the union of marriage) can have in the Kingdom of God!!! "Synergism" is defined by Webster as the "cooperative action of discrete agencies such that the total effect is greater than the sum of the effects taken independently." In other words, one may have two different chemicals that aren't much in themselves alone, but when combined, may have incredible and powerful results. So it is also for two people who are one in Christ in the sexual bond in marriage. There takes place the inextricable intermingling, synergistically, of soul and spirit that produces unbelievably positive results for the Kingdom of God!!! The Bible tells us how should "one chase a thousand, and two put ten thousand to flight" (Deut.32:30.) Jesus said, "Again I say unto you, That if two of you shall agree on earth as touching any thing that they shall ask, it shall be done for them of My Father which is in heaven." (Matt.18:19). Do you see the synergism?

RESTORATION & HEALING

Please understand that one has nothing personal against the one being "quarantined". But what is the proper course when one repents and wants to be restored? It is entirely inappropriate for others to "remember", when God forgets. And it is wrong for us to consider others as "second class citizens of the Kingdom", whom God has restored and forgiven. There are several Scriptures that deal with this:

In I Corinthians, the Apostle Paul "sets an immoral Christian outside the Body of Christ". But in II Corinthians, Paul encourages them to forgive and restore:

"Sufficient to such a man is this punishment, which was inflicted of many. So that contrariwise ye ought rather to forgive him, and comfort him, lest perhaps such an one be swallowed up with overmuch sorrow. Wherefore I beseech you that ye would confirm your love toward him....To whom ye forgive anything, I forgive also: for if I forgave anything, to whom I forgave it, for your sakes forgave I it in the person of

254

Christ...Now thanks be unto Christ who ALWAYS causes us to triumph in Christ, and maketh manifest the savor of His knowledge by us in EVERY PLACE." II Corinthians 2:6,7,8,10,14.

SYMPATHY, or "SYMPATHY"

Suppose there are three people walking down the street. Let's say that the first one falls down of a heart attack. Then the second person sees what happens and feels such commiserating, empathetic, pitying, compassionate, heart- felt sympathy, that he or she goes into hysterics, screams and cries, goes into shock and falls beside the first one in a swoon or a faint, unconscious. Then the third person almost gruffly shoulders through the crowd, pushes them back, orders a person to call the ambulance, makes the first victim comfortable, jerks open his tie and shirt, ministers mouth to mouth "rescuperation", and CPR massage, sees the ambulance on its way, and then calmly straightens out his own tie and walks on down the street. In all this time, he had no worries, sweat or tears.

Question: In this above example, which of the last two people had the most compassion or sympathy or commiseration or empathy or love?

One of the greatest deterrants to seeing people helped, is that kind of sick "sympathy" that is weak-kneed, sissyfied, "sob sistered", crippling, and ineffective - even contributing to the problem.

There is an interesting Scripture from Proverbs (19:18) that says, "Chasten thy son while there is

255

hope, and let not thy soul spare for his crying." And again in Prov.13:24, "He that spareth (or fails to use) his rod, (or flexible whipping switch), hateth his son: but he that loveth him chasteneth him betimes (or: from time to time)".(Also 22:15; 23:13,14; & 29:15,17.)

"MINISTER TO ME ON MY TERMS!"

There is much pressure usually brought to bear on the counsellor by people who want to be ministered to on their terms. Often, they will not only have their problem seemingly properly defined, but they will insist that they know the solution as well, and they want you to give it to them. The kid who wants lots of candy thinks that his problem is lack of candy and that the solution to his problem is lots of candy, and now! So, the pressure is on. The counsellor must objectively look to the Lord to see just what the problem is in the first place, and what the solution is in the second. If Jesus would have healed Lazarus instead of raising him from the dead, He would have failed to do His Father's will. The family and the disciples thought that the problem was a sick man who simply needed to be healed. But Jesus knew that the sick man needed to die! The pressure was on. His dear friends said, "If You had come, Lazarus would not have died!"

SPIRITUAL PROSTITUTION

If a counsellor yields to the pressure to compromise and conform, and sometimes the pressure is great, then that counsellor is a spiritual prostitute. And spiritual prostitution is the worst prostitution of all. Often the counselee says, "Look, if you don't agree with my definition of the problem and the solution and if you don't give it to me, I'll stop being your friend, or quit the church, or be angry with you, or stop giving money to you," etc.

INFANT EXTORTION

Have you ever heard a 6 months old baby say to himself something like this: "Even though I've been held, bounced, burped, blessed, changed and fed; and even though Mommy laid me down for a nap, I have in fact, decided that my problem is that I need to be held, the solution is for Mom to hold me right now, and I'm going to lay here and scream and fuss and cry and wail and yell and kick my feet and clench my fists, and grit my gums, and whimper and sob and contort my face until I make everybody so miserable that they'll have absolutely no choice but to pamper me and let me have my baby way back to bountiful bosom base." But the sad fact is that some people get by with this kind of extortion and blackmail well into adulthood and now must learn that God and His representatives will not yield to these extortion attempts. Counsellors become spiritual prostitutes if they give in to the temptation that says, "I will pay you (in favor, friendship, tithes, etc.), if you give me the satisfaction I crave." (If you are interested, see our book, *How To Raise "Purfect" Kids).*

The prophets and men and women of God have always faced this pressure that demands, "Give me a word from God that I want you to give to me, that satisfies me, and I won't persecute you."

Therefore, in the same way God does with us, we must always act in one another's BEST interest. We must never minister to any one on their terms, and never on our terms, but always on God's terms.

PHONEY PHONING

Jesus must be Lord of all that we say or think or are or do. Our use of the telephone is an example. A friend called today that owed us some money. I did not have the time, nor did I feel the leading to talk to this person, so I gave Joshua the message to give, that I did not have the time to talk. The caller replied to him, "If he doesn't have time to talk, then he can forget his money that I have for him." I told Joshua to say, "O.K., Goodbye!" and hang up. Now you may think that this is cold blooded and cruel. But either you have Jesus Christ as your Lord or you have the telephone as your lord. If Jesus is your Lord, then He decides if, or who, you talk to about what and for how long!!! But you may say, "Yes, but I don't want to offend anyone!" But who would you rather offend, your friend, or your Friend the Lord??? Many people actually choose to offend the Lord than to offend people! Strange, but true! Reminds me of a driver who would rather miss a little doggie, squirrel or kitty cat and hit a tree, and kill their whole family because of a misdirected and sick sense of sympathy. And this is also the case where spiritual and Scriptural quarantine are needed, but they would rather expose the family of God and their own family to hideous contamination to keep from being "mean" to a poor little critter.

YOU AIN'T BLED YET!

I have a friend who has a pet little sin or two that he just loves to play with and pamper. But then he gets a guilty conscience. He likes to smoke pot and love Jesus at the same time, but then he gets upset with ministries because they don't give him the "magic" solution. He dares them to give him the solution, but when they even start to begin to commence to apply "tuff luv" he wails and raves like a cat with its tail in the door. His least favorite Scripture seems to be, "Ye have not yet resisted unto blood, striving against sin." Hebrews 12:4.

When I was in Brazil ministering, I heard a true story about a snake whose bite is so deadly that it usually kills within a few seconds. One day a man was cutting his way through the jungle when one of these vipers bit him in the hand. There was no hesitation whatsoever - no deliberation, no debate, no indecision. His machete sword knife was in his other hand. It was - bite - swing - CHOP!!! Off came his arm! Do you think this was cold-blooded? It was DO or DIE! And to die is even more "cold blooded". When Jesus says in Mark 9:43, "When thy hand offend thee, cut it off," what He really meant was that we need to really "get tough" with ourselves and stop doing the offending thing, or else cut off the offending member. But no, we have been babied, pampered, "namby-pambied", "moddy-coddled", weak kneed, sissyfied and spoiled even to the point where we would rather enter hell whole than to enter heaven maimed.

Please understand, we are NOT against the person, any more than a family would be against a quarantined child. But we INSIST, in these clear-cut cases of spiritual quarantine, that the person, sincerely repent, AND be totally delivered from the sin and its bondage, before the quarantine is lifted, and the person be restored to fellowship. Can you see how love must be the motive?

OLD TESTAMENT EXAMPLES

There are those who have been taught that God is not mean or cruel, and that He is always nice and is sometimes a sissy. But the fact is that if you read the Bible with an open heart about this, without twisting the Scripture, you will surely discover that Jesus Christ is still the same today as He was in the days of old.

I know that the Old Testament is old, but it still is an indication to us of what God still thinks of sin. He hasn't changed His mind about its awfulness. Jesus Christ is still the same today, as He was in the Old Testament!!! (Did you know that He existed before He was born in Bethleham? John 1 says that "In the beginning" Jesus created everything "that was made".) He chased Adam from the Garden, cut Cain off from his family, cut man off from the earth, destroyed Sodom and Gomorrah, and the first born in

Egypt. Then He killed Nadab and Abihu with fire, Korah with the swallowing up of the earth, and killed the rebellious Israelites with the plague, etc. God honored and blessed Phinehas: for executing the couple while they were fornicating, Samuel: for chopping Agag to pieces, also the priest: for cutting up his concubine, Elijah: for calling down fire and Elijah: for calling out the bears on the children, and for calling up leprosy on Gehazi. (See our article that we have written about "Hell".)

NEW TESTAMENT EXAMPLES

Jesus drove out the money changers, Paul struck Elymas blind, Peter saw Ananias and Sapphira drop dead, the two Men of God killed people with fire out of their mouth. The Book of Revelation sees the judgements of God dropping 100 pound hailstones on peoples's heads, earthquakes destroying every major city, 1/3 and 2/3'rds of the earth's population killed, and blood running as high as the bridle of a horse for a distance of 200 miles!

JESUS IS LORD

The whole key to this, as with everything, is that God has a right to be God! And God is looking for those who will obey Him. We are like concerned relatives who run into the operating room of God when the Great Physician is performing a delicate operation. There are two dangers: the one is to grab God's Hand and say, "Thrust the knife deeper." And the other is to say, "Not so deep, not so deep."

THE CIRCLE OF GOD

Imagine, if you will, a circle that represents every thing that is included in the perfect will of God. As we explain in detail in our book about marriage, called *The Sexual Ministry,* legalism and religiosity exists when we draw the circle of morality and behavior tighter than God does, and make things illegal that God says nothing about. For example, the Bible does NOT say, "Thou shalt NOT kiss her there!" (This book on marriage explains how to hang up our ungodly hangups). On the other hand licentiousness, greasy "grace" and sloppy agape exist when we draw the circle looser than God does; and we become out of balance, the extent to which we draw the circle "other than" God does.

FALSE DOCTRINES

When we do this with the Word of God, false doctrines result. The Church has allowed elaborate false doctrines, from "greasy grace" and "sloppy agape" and infernal security and ultimate recon- ciliation, on the one hand, to that legalism and religiosity on the other that has people going to hell for spitting on the side-walk or stepping on the cracks! Some people have God looking at our sins through the blood colored glasses of Jesus (or Mary -take your pick), to the point where He can't even see our sin. This is spastic silliness, because God sees us as we are. If we sin God knows it and will judge us for it, if we do not repent. And if we repent, God doesn't see it any more cause it "ain't" there any more.

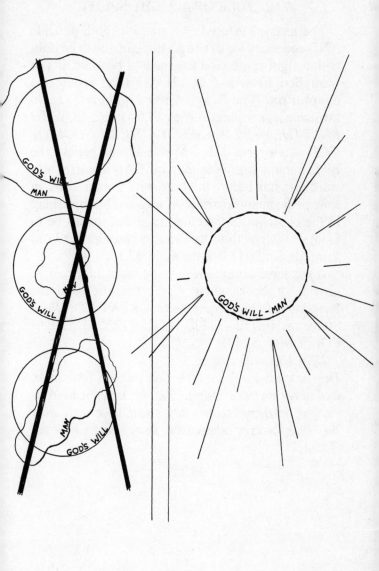

THE RULE OF A RIGHT SPIRIT

The truth of the matter is that it is both possible AND necessary for us to both do right and to be right with a right spirit. God has made it possible. If you want Scriptures and details on this, review the chapter on "The King's Greatest Secret", (also available as a separate article), Our book, *HOW TO RULE THE WORLD or SEEK 1st THE KINGDOM OF GOD!* is also available. Also, read and believe the Bible's many promises that we CAN consistently walk pleasing before the Lord with a right heart, in spite of the many doctrinal excuses and brainwashing in the churches to the contrary. "But thanks be to God, which giveth us the victory through our Lord Jesus Christ!!!" (I Corinthians 15:57.)

If you have a question or desire more information, articles or books about God's Priorities and the Kingdom of God, please write: GREAT COMMISSION MINISTRIES, P.O. BOX 7123, MINNEAPOLIS, MN., 55407.

Dear Heavenly Father,
Help us to always relate to the dear ones on Your terms, and never on ours. Help us that we agree with Your circle of behavior and morality, and that we never draw the circle for us or others, other than You do. In Jesus' Name.

AMEN.

CHAPTER 12 - REVIEW

1. What do we mean "Kingdom Quarantine"?
2. List some situations where you think Scriptural quarantine is recommended:
3. What specific methods of quarantine does the Scripture call for?
4. What should our attitude be toward someone on quarantine?
5. What do we mean "relate to someone on their terms"?
6. What do we mean "phoney phoning"?
7. What do we mean by "inextricable intermingling"?
8. How can the "bond" be broken?
9. When should the quarantine be lifted?
10. Describe the difference between sympathy and empathy, as we have defined them.
11. Is it possible for one to always keep a right heart attitude or spirit?
12. What do we mean "infant extortion"?
13. What do we mean "Spiritual prostitution"?
14. Describe at least 4 New Testament examples of "Tuff Luv".
15. What is the verse that essentially says, "YOU ain't bled yet"?
16. What do we mean "Synergism"?
17. What is it called when we draw the circle of morality larger than God does?
18. Or when we draw the circle tighter than God?
19. What are we when the circle is "other than" God's?

CHAPTER 13 — OUTLINE

SEDUCTION

I. First Letter to Hunt & McMahon
II. Second Leter to Hunt & McMahon
III. Conclusion
IV. What Do You Think
V. Review

13

SEDUCTION!!!

Dear Readers: Before we bring this book to a close, we thought that it would be good to respond to a book that relates to this whole issue of cannibalism in the Body of Christ. This chapter is kind of like a classroom or laboratory where a classical example of "Christian" cannibalism is presented and studied.

As you will see, we have very carefully followed the protocol and procedures outlined in Scripture in dealing with this kind of subject matter. We have encouraged you also to follow the Lord's way of dealing with disagreements, and divisions in Christ's Body. We will give some comments and explanations, after the letters.

We wanted to include, for your benefit, an open letter to the authors of the book, *THE SEDUCTION OF CHRISTIANITY*. Let it be known that we have very carefully followed the Scriptural rules of protocol in a situation like this. Here is what we have done:

#1. First we VERY VERY carefully, prayerfully and reverently analyzed and studied the material.

#2. Then, I called the Christian Information Bureau on "Mockingbird" Lane in Dallas, and talked to a man there named "Jay". I asked for the authors' addresses, and was told that they were taking all of their correspondence through the "Mockingbird" address. Jay promised me that if I wrote to them there, that he would faithfully send all of the material to them. I told him that I would be sending this following letter to them, at the address Jay gave me, and that if I did not receive a letter back from them, that I would be writing a second time.

#3. I then sent to authors Hunt and McMahon the following letter, and a copy of my first book, *HOW TO RULE THE WORLD, or SEEK 1st THE KINGDOM OF GOD.* I also sent a copy of my book to Jay.

#4. That first letter was sent on January 10, 1986. My call to Jay was made even before that. BUT I RECEIVED NO REPLY OR ACKNOWLEDGMENT OF ANY KIND. Then, after 8 weeks, I decided to write again. This time I wrote another letter, which is also included here. I also included a copy of my first letter, when I sent to them my second. I mentioned, as you can see, that if I did not hear some kind of acknowledgment from the authors of *SEDUCTION,* that the next time they heard from me would be here, in this book. Let me explain why:

Jesus says in Matthew 18 these words:

"Moreover if thy brother shall trespass against thee, GO AND TELL HIM his fault between thee and him alone: IF HE SHALL HEAR THEE, thou hast gained thy brother."

"But IF HE WILL NOT HEAR THEE, then take one or two more, that in the mouth of two or three witnesses, every word may be established."

"And IF HE SHALL NEGLECT TO HEAR them, TELL IT UNTO THE CHURCH: but IF HE NEGLECT TO HEAR THE CHURCH, LET HIM BE UNTO THEE AS AN HEATHEN MAN AND A PUBLICAN."

#5. This time I got a response, not from the authors, but from Jay. He tried to answer some of the questions, and promised me that McMahon would reply, but that Hunt was "too busy", and Hunt said that I should do what I felt that I "had to do".

#6. The Bible says, that "If they will not listen" that we should "tell it to the Church". This is the manner that I have chosen to "tell it to the church". So, now, after almost a year after my first letter, I still have not heard from either of the authors of *Seduction.*

Here then, are my open letters to them and my concluding remarks about this seduction:

1/10/86

To: Dave Hunt & T.A. Mc Mahon
c/o Christian Information Bureau
6102 East Mockingbird Lane #231
Dallas, Texas 75214

Regarding: *The Seduction Of Christianity —*
Spiritual Discernment In The Last Days

Dear Brothers Hunt & Mc Mahon:

It was most enjoyable to talk to Jay at your headquarters there in Dallas. He seemed extremely helpful, kind and co-operative. He also assured me that you are very approachable and have a very teachable heart. Perhaps we can reason together.

I have read your book very very carefully & prayerfully, and I have felt responsible to write to you some things I feel are important before the Lord Jesus. I hope that you can find the time to respond, in spite of your busy schedule.

I have been in two meetings where this book has been discussed, but since I have only now read the book, am only now responding.

First, let me say that there is much, much of what you say that I find agreement with. In fact, I have written a book about cults that will soon be published. I want to compliment you on your extensive research that you obviously have done. I would like to have your permission to quote back to you several passages that you have written in your book, beginning with my very favorite portion, that I agree with & like the most: "What counts is our love for Him, [Christ], our simple faith in His word, and our obedience to the leading of His spirit in the present. The secret to Joy and fruitfulness as a Christian is our dynamic relationship to Christ living in our hearts right now." p.187.

My heart also has joy at your statement on that page that "Christ is our life"!!! In my book which I am sending you, Please see Chapter 7, page 77 on "The King's Greatest Secret", where I talk about Jesus Christ actually being our Life!

I also specifically agree with you on the following:

1. That the Bible must be our guide book, compass and plumbline in all matters; it of course, is God's inspired & infallible word to us.

2. That there definitely are excesses and wrong teachings in some of the movements that you describe — in contrast, I believe that: A. We **can** "pray the problem", B. Prosperity must be used for the fulfillment of the Great Commission, C. All that we claim by faith in Christ, must be according to His will, and not our own, D. Financial prosperity is not necessarily a sign of God's favor, E. That we'll not catch a cold just because we have a negative thought.

3. That we must never open ourselves to demons;

4. That death to self is necessary for discipleship;

5. That we can't send Mary or Joseph to do the Lord's work;

6. That experience and psychological theories are not self authenticating, but that the Bible is;

7. That digging up the past, or "Trips into the past" are often unnecessary for healing;

8. That "The entire Bible must be studied as a unit";

9. That Jesus Christ is Lord.

I have some questions for you:

I. Did you make any attempt to plead with, reason with, communicate with, rebuke, exhort, or get any explanations from any of the brethren that you quoted — especially Capps, Copeland, Hagin, Tilton, Cho, Zig, Bennets, Wimber, Etc.??? The Bible says, "Rebuke not an elder, but **go to Him**"!!! Did you go to them? Bible says, "If your brother offends you , **Go to him**"!!! Bible says, "Do you see your brother in a fault? then **go to him**"!!! (They said no!)

God has a plan whereby we can see our brother restored, and if we don't follow His plan, then untold damage can happen in the body of Christ, through our "sowing of discord among the brethren". Matthew 18:15 — "and if your brother sins, go and reprove him in private; if he listens to you, you have won your brother. But if he does not listen to you, take one or two more with you, so that by the mouth of two or three witnesses every fact may be confirmed. And if he refuses to listen to them, **tell it to the Church...**"

II. Question: Did you follow this process before you "Told it to the Church"??? I need to know, for if you did not, then I believe you are wrong, and need to repent. And if you don't repent, then I need to "tell it to the church". I plan to come to you a second time though. If I get no response from you, I'll assume that you are "refusing to listen" to me. (VSS. 15,16 & 17.) (please read)

I had a problem with Bro. Hagin one time. He did something that offended me, and of which I disapproved. But rather than sow discord among the brethren, or book bite against him I chose to "go to him", by way of a letter like this. He doesn't know me any better than you do, but a short time later, here came a letter from him in which: #1, he explained his point of view in a non-defensive, non-self-vindicating way, and #2, he apologized to me and repented for what he did, and #3, He asked me to forgive him.

So, the question that I have, is, did you go to any of these brothers in an attempt to "restore them in a spirit of meekness, considering yourselves, lest you also be tempted."??? (They admitted they had not!)

It was explained to me that you sometimes excuse yourself from following these biblical **mandates** for reconciliation and restoration in the body of Christ because:

A. "The ministry they shared was 'public', therefore the correction can come publicly." (Though you may have a point here, I know that in my own ministry, I don't know all that there is to know about God yet, and rather than have my ministry in the Lord be publicly discredited, I like to be first told in private, so that I can have a chance to get on my face before God about the matter, and then, if God so directs, make public correction and apology.) How would you personally like to be treated in this regard??? I know that the Scriptures say, "Them that sin, rebuke before all, that the rest may fear." There is such a weight of truth that speaks of going directly to the person first, or at least of making the attempt. There is something clean, honorable, kind, loving, considerate about the attempt to privately correct — first. Then if they will not hear...

B. It was also said in your defense that it would be difficult for you to go to all the people you quote. I agree that it would definitely take some work. I personally have spent the better part of the last 4 days and nights preparing this appeal to you, and although I may only get a tearing and a trampling for my trouble, I love you enough to make the attempt, and I love the Lord's ways of reconciliation, unity and restoration.

C. Again, it was said, that often the leaders are unapproachable, and cannot be reached, or communicated with, or are otherwise unresponsive. I'll admit that this, too can be a problem, but at least you would have attempted to do the honorable thing, and would have done your part to be fair.

D. It was mentioned that often the leaders are unteachable, become angry, fly into a rage — but again you are not responsible for their reaction, only to make the first and second appeal. The Bible says, "If they won't listen... then tell it to the Church."

Now, let us get into the book itself, for there are some places that I believe, if you are teachable, that like Apollo, you can be "shown a better way". Or

III. Do you already know all that there is to know about God???

IV. Are you teachable? You mentioned that these people, whose teachings you criticize, "are accountable to no one but themselves", and are "insulated from any correction..." please let me ask you, to whom are *you* accountable??? I am interested to know if *you* are also "insulated from correction"? I am goint to find our if *you* are teachable, and if *you* really believe the Bible where it says, "let the righteous smite me, it shall be considered a kindness." & "he that rebukes, afterward finds more favor than he that flatters with the tongue." & "Faithful are the wounds of a friend," & "Rebuke a wise man, and he

274

will love thee." Let's see if you are wise. Let's see if you are approachable. Let's see if you can be reasoned with. Let's see if you can hear God speak to you through this donkey.

V. Why did you not define the following terms, because I believe these definitions are important for us to know where you are coming from?:

1. "Cult",

2. "Occult" (Someone who believes different from you?),

3. "MYSTICISM" - Is there no such thing as "Christian mysticism"? viz. Brother Lawrence, Madame Guyone, Apostle Paul, (Caught up into the 7th heaven and given things unlawful for man to utter) etc. I have found that there are among Christian circles, valid definitions of the word mysticism that, within the framework of that valid definition, there definitely is such a thing as a valid Christian Mysticism. In fact, I would say, that in the common vernacular, that Paul, Daniel, Ezekiel, Apostle John, and others who have had dreams and visions, etc., are considered valid Christian mystics, simply because they have had Godly and righteous supernatural experiences with God.

By certain people's definition though, this causes people to see all kinds of dangers. Just because there are some witches and devil worshippers, and navel contemplators who call themselves "mystics" doesn't have to mess the word up for me. I simply inquire where the dear one is coming from. That is the real issue — the source! Some people are so terrified of anything supernatural, that they want to scare every-one else from reaching into God for the things that really really **are** from Him. I believe, that the proper course is for us to teach the dear ones how to discern, how to know right from wrong, the true from the false, how to try spirits, rather than discourage them from seeking, and waiting on God, through Jesus Christ & His blood.

4. "Visualization", (I read pp.123 & 124, but are not the following Scriptural examples of a kind of visualizing, that God wants of us?

A. "**Looking** unto Jesus, the author and finisher...";

B. "I do only what I **see** the Father doing.." JN.5:30;

C. "While **beholding** Him... into the very same image!";

D. "As a man **thinketh in his heart,** so is he.";

E. "Whatsoever things are lovely..**think on these**.."

F. "While **seeing** Him Who was invisible...";

G. "Set your affections on things that are above...";

H. "**Remember** the prophesies spoken over your life, and govern your life by them...";

I. "Believe that you have the petitions, and you shall..." etc.

5. "Success" — you kept putting it down. Are you against success in Christ in our victory, fruitfulness and conquering?

6. "Meditation" — "In His law doth He **meditate,** day and night", etc. This word is mentioned 20 times in the Bible in a Godly sense! I believe that our refusal to meditate on God and His precepts is the problem!

7. "Paradigm Shift", you take Wimber to task for this on p. 174, but I missed the definition somewhere.

8. "gods" — Bible uess the word "elohiym" often to describe something living and good, other than God or YahwEH.

VI. In your book, why did you seem to totally ignore a whole segment of truth portrayed by those whose teachings you criticize? The implication by inference is that there is no "other side to the question". For example, what do we do with scriptures like "All things are possible to him that believes." and "If two of you agree as touching anything.. I will do it." and "Life and death is in the power of the tongue" and "We have the mind of Christ" and "Whatsoever is...of good report, think on these things," and "Love always belives that best about each situation," and "To the pure all things are pure" and "As a man thinketh...so is he." and "According to your faith be it unto you," and "Nothing shall be impossible to him that believes" and "The greater works", etc., etc., etc. It seems that you have taken the teaching (not the quotes, but the teaching), of these dear ones often out of context, and have neither dealt with nor answered the truth these Scriptures present. The Scriptures on **all** sides of the argument must be agreed on.

VII. Have you torn up the wheat with the tares? Pray about it.

VIII. A good example of this, and, I suppose, another question is, why do you lump the good with the bad so closely? For example, on page 97, in the same paragraph, you have lumped Hagin, Copeland

and Capps in with cults, mind-science and the occult!!! Are you inferring or stating that Copeland, Hagin and Capps are devil worshippers, sorcerers, or witches?

IX. Are you aware that blaspheming the Holy Spirit is that unforgivable sin of attributing to satan that which is of the Spirit of God?? Sorcery is forgivable — this sin is not! Guilty?

X. Are you aware of the Bible principle of "Touching the Lord's anointed"? The "anointed" that David refused to touch was A. demon possessed, B. a liar, C. a murderer, D. a consulter or a witch. Is it possible that you have "touched" the anointed of God that are neither liars, witch consulters, murderers or devil possessed? Bible says, "Touch not mine anointed, and do my prophets no harm." I know that Wimber, Copeland, Hagin, Bennets, Wilkerson, Cho, Capps, etc. do not know all that there is to know about God yet, and that they "know and prophesy in part", but I am not aware that any of them are liars, witch consulters, murderers or demon possessed. Yet, do you "touch" them? Do you put them into the same bag with the occultists, the cultists and the mind scientists??? Perhaps the Lord will use your own yardstick on you, and put you into the same bag with the "touchers of the Lord's anointed," the slanderers, the sowers of discord among the brethren, the blasphemers of the Holy Spirit???

XI. You take a crack at the "manifested sons of God". Is this another "boogey man" that you are "hunt"ing? or do you believe Romans 8 after all? You said that you wanted to avoid theological "hair splitting". Why would you limit how great God wants to make Himself in us? A lot of theological hair got split, and before God, it's all numbered!

XII. Do you think it is possible that you miss the point entirely of the test question that satan put to Eve in the garden??? Let's look at the possibility that the issue was not whether or not they would be as gods, but the means to being or becoming these gods, (with a small 'g'). Look at the overwhelming preponderance of evidence — that the Psalmist and Jesus really meant what they said when they said, "Ye are gods"! & that the Scriptures actually mean what they say, when they say, "As He is, so are we in this world!" and "walk as He walked" and "partakers of the divine nature", and "In His image" and 2 Cor.3:18, "The very same image"! Is it possible that here you throw the baby out too? Doesn't the existence of a counterfeit dollar bill only prove the existence of a real one? On p.83, I cannot tell the difference between the "image" and the "exact duplicate", though you describe the distance between them as a "quantum leap".

If Christ becomes our Life, and "For me to live is Christ" and He's living His life through me, is it not true that the Christ, Who is my Life, is God? "If they hear you they hear *Me*", "Saul, why do you persecute *Me?*" And "Inasmuch as you have done it unto them...you did it unto Me?" Is it *possible* that you are lacking a revelation of the Scriptures in this regard??? Time after time the word "gods" (Hebrew = Elohiym), is used to describe a living and acceptable entity. "God is not the God of the dead, but of the living"! Time after time Yahweh is referred to as being the "Lord God of gods" or the "Yahwey El of eloihm" viz. Joshua 22:22. The fact that Yahweh and Yeshuah is the Lord of lords, the King of kings, and God of gods, doesn't make God any less Yahweh nor me any less human. He delights in making trophies of triumph of all who are willing.

Isn't it possible that God **intended** for man to occupy a god-ly place with Him on His throne, to qualify for this place on God's terms, in God's time, in God's way, but that satan was trying to offer a "short cut", as was the case at the temptation of Christ, "If You fall down and worship me, I will give You all these worlds to rule over." Just because satan asked the question or made the offer doesn't mean that it was not God's ultimate intent. It was the will of the Father for Christ to rule these nations, but in Father's way & time, etc."

Isn't it also the will of God for us "to rule over the nations with a rod of iron", and to exercise our responsibilities to "bind and loose", & to "agree as touching", & to "bind the kings with chains, the nobles with fetters of iron, execute vengeance on the nations, punishments on the people and execute upon them the judgement written? (Psalm 149)? Isn't it time for us to "take the Kingdom by force"? (Jesus). Daniel 7: "And the time came when the Saints took possession of the Kingdom!"??? Don't you agree, that **you also** should "study the entire Bible as a unit."??

XIII. Is it not true after all that God is, in a very real sense, bound by His own nature and character as God to act as God??? For example, the Bible says, "God is not a man, that He should lie.." apparently, then, God cannot lie can He? Throughout the book, you keep making the point that God is not bound by laws, or even cause and effect principals, that it must be all by "grace", or God wouldn't be God. But what about His gracious covenant relationship with us??? Isn't it true that every gracious promise He makes to us, He binds Himself into keeping His part of the "bargain" or agreement, if you will??? Is this Plymouth Brethren?

You make the inference that He is above His own law or it wouldn't be grace, or something to this effect. For example, on page 97, where you lump Hagin, Copeland & Capps into the same paragragh with cult, occult & your cult, oops, strike the words "your cult", & mind science, you state: "yet many Christians make God Himself subject to law without realizing that they have destroyed Him in the process; for who needs God if everything happens according to laws that even God must obey? This eliminates true miracles and ...and turns prayer into a technique for releasing divine power by following certain principles, rather than submitting to God's will and trusting His wisdom, love and grace."

XIV. Isn't it true that we are always under some kind of "law"? Bible says, "the **law of the Spirit of life in Christ Jesus** has set me free from the law of sin and death." Isn't there also the law of love? Isn't it true that every word God speaks, and every promise He

281

makes, every covenant He establishes, that He Himself submits Himself to keeping "His side" of it??? Makes no difference if it is called a law or a promise, hasn't God "obligated Himself" to be true to His own nature and character, by keeping His own promise??? I John 1:9, "**If** we confess our sins..." "**If** two of you agree..."; "I assure you, most solemnly I tell you, **if** any one steadfastly believes in Me, he will himself be able to do the things that I do; and he will do even greater things than these, because I go to the Father." (John 14:12), or is God entitled to say, "Because I am God, I don't have to be true to My word."? The Bible says, "He has said, and will He not do it? He hath spoken, and shall He not make it good?" Yet you seem to indicate that one who takes God at His word or "follows the rules" in this way is — a **sorcerer???**

XV. on p.151, you state that, "new thought became the basis for such mind-science cults as Christian Science..." and went on to say "...new thought survived... in extreme Pentecostalism and in organizations like..." My question for you is this, what are you a "fightin' fundy"??? Anit-Pentecostalist??? Every time you mention tongues, it is in a spastic context. I am not in favor of Peal's pantheism, nor of Grubb's every body is God, nor of Schuller's zen buddhism, etc., but are you suggesting that we substitute positive thinking for negative thinking, pma for a negative mentality, faith for unbelief, aggressively occupying 'til He comes for a sick and passive Christian country club nirvanna?

XVI. Is it not true that in one sense our own new man's "human potential" is fully acutalized when Christ becomes our Life, and when we do His will to the supernatural maximum, by His spirit, through His power, for His glory???

XVII. On p.99 you seem to teach against the "power inherent within words". Perhaps the Lord will "bonk" you with the same yardstick measure that you yourselves use to spank the Lord's anointed, "but the word of God is quick and powerful, and sharper than any two-edged sword. Piercing..." Should we throw it away?

XVIII. Brothers, I believe you missed the whole point, and wrote large portions of your book about an issue that has as a broken leg. Your concept on p.101, "there is **no** cause and effect relationship between.. man and God;". Before God, you are wrong, wrong, wrong, wrong, wrong wrong wrong!!!!!! Not only are you wrong, but you call those that do teach this Kingdom Principle: witch doctors, rooster killers, magicians, and the tripe. Again, I say: **every** promise God makes, **every** invitation He gives, **every** prayer He invites us to pray, **every** word He commands us to speak, involves a cause and effect relationship!!! God says, "**Ask** of Me, **and I will......**", "**Give,** and **it shall be...**", "**Bind,** and **it shall be...**", "**Ask,** and **it shall be...**", "**If** any man will open the door, **I will....**", "**If** two of you ageee...." talk about cause and effect!!! "Delight **thyself** in Me, **and I will...**", "**If** we confess our sins...", "The soul that sinneth, it shall...", "**Believe on** the Lord Jesus Christ, **and thou shalt be...**" You end that chapter on p.104 by saying "that is the issue". We must always have control, even in our yielding to Him. "The spirit of the prophets is subject to the prophets." We had better maintain control, under God's control, or the enemy will. I agree that we must **never** use or try to manipulate God, to our selfish ends, and your point is well taken here, but we absolutely **must** do some naming and claiming under His orders, in His time and for His glory!!! Are you stubbornly set into an "ultra-sovereignty-of-God" doctrine?? Someone said that it would never occur to you that you could be wrong about anything. Is this true or are you teachable?

Now I close with a word about witch *"hunt-ing"* and cult finding.

1. Historically, that which God did in one generation almost always has persecuted that which God did in the next generation.

2. "Those who live Godly...shall suffer persecution."

3. "A man's foes shall be they of **his own household.**"

4. They will kill Christians, **thinking** they did **God's will!**

5. "**Had they known,** they would not have crucified ..."

6. They called the early Christians "Heretics". Acts 24:14.

7. They crucified Jesus because **they thought He was cultic.**

8. Jesus said, "I have many things to tell you, but you are not able to bear it." Sometimes we criticize others

because we don't know yet what they have been shown. (Fear of the unknown).

9. If Christ Himself could not pass the test of a critical spirit, neither will His servants. His family thought Him insane!

10. A deceived man **never** knows when He's deceived.

11. You may be interested in the following series, as I find that folks constantly get these things confused. We all need to identify approximately what it is, where it is on this list?

(1). Of the devil (2). Blasphemy (3). Heresy (4). Cultic (5). False Doctrine (6). A lie (7). Deception (8). Occultic (9). Exlusivistic (10). Wrong Doctrine (11). Foolishness (12). Didn't say it right (13). Immaturity (14). Mistakes (15). None of my business (16). A guess (17). An estimate (18). A theory (19). Opinion-"I think". (20). "Feel a check" (21). Differing opinion (22). Perspective: 2 sided coin or 5 blind men describing elephant (23). Something I havne't learned, yet — Jealous or critical (24). Thought (25). Conviction (26). Belief (27). Fact (28). Reality (29). Truth (30). Thus saith the Lord (31). God doesn't want me to know it yet

I've seen well meaning Christians say something was of the devil, when in fact, it was a "thus saith the Lord" — God's truth — that they just had't been shown yet. These "well-meaners" may have blasphemed the Holy Spirit by attributing to satan that which really was of God! Isn't this what "blaspheming the Holy Spirit" means to you? (Mark chapter 3).

285

I am enclosing a book which I have written. I do so with Godly fear and trembling, because I don't know if you will turn and hurt me, through negative publicity or slander. I know already, though from what you have said, that you do not yet know the truth of what God says in His word about some of the things I deal with in my book, concerning our victory in Christ. But I cast myself upon your mercy, and upon the mercy of God. I am willing to be taught by the Christ through you, but I am not masochistically desiring your public mutilation or dismembering.

When my book on the cults comes out, I plan that you will have a copy. The next couple of weeks will determine whether or not you are mentioned in it, and how. Please respond teachably. Please.

I count you as better than myself. I love you. I hope that we can meet. I hope that we can be good friends in the will of God.

My phone number is 612-823-1783. You are welcome to call me any time of the night or day, with rebukes, corrections, suggestions, questions or for prayer or encouragement. No mutilation, please!

"Until we all come to the unity of the faith............"

John Roy Bohlen,
P.O. 7123,
Minneapolis, MN. 55407

3/7/86

TO: Dave Hunt & T.A. Mc Mahon
c/o Christian Information Bureau
6102 East Mockingbird Lane #231
Dallas, Texas 75214

Regarding: *The Seduction of Christianity —
Spiritual Discernment in the Last Days*

Dear Brothers Hunt & Mc Mahon:

Greetings to you in the mighty name of Jesus, Who is our Lord & Who is come in the flesh!!!

This is not the second time I am coming to you, actually the third. If you don't respond to this one, the next word you will have from me will be in a book I am writing called, *The Cult of Cannibals,* in which I talk frankly about the rank murder that is done by believers to each other in the sweet Name of Jesus. I'll even send you a copy. Did you get my first letter and book, entitled, *How to Rule the World?* No one has acknowledged it if you did.

Also, for your benefit, I am enclosing a copy of my first letter from you, in case you did not receive the first.

My phone number is 612-823-1783. You are welcome to call my any time of the night or day, with rebukes, corrections, suggestions, questions or for prayer and encouragement. No mutilation, Please!

"Until we all come to the unity of the faith............"

John Roy Bohlen, P.O. 7123,
Minneapolis, MN. 55407

CONCLUSION

Well, dear reader, there you have it. We understand that authors Hunt or McMahon made ABSOLUTELY NO EFFORT TO CONTACT THE PEOPLE THEY CRITICIZED!!! It it precisely because of this kind of horribly destructive cannibalism that we have written this book.

We discovered that the main author, David Hunt, comes from a strong predestination, almost fatalism, sovereignty of God, fundamentalist, dispensationalist background that, as he states in his book, leaves NO room for a meaningful cause and effect relationship with God!!! Therefore, those who dare to "take God at His Word" and enter in to take advantage of God's Promises, are suspect.

Hunt's treatment of those who believe that God can make us like Him, is terrifying. Oh God, please help us to love each other!!!

This cannibalistic and seductive book is, ironically, called, *The Seduction of Christianity*. We do NOT recommend the book, unless you are in a position where you need to "intelligently" counsel those who have read it or those who are thinking of reading it.

If you do want to have more information about this book of seduction, we recommend the book, SEDUCTION?? A BIBLICAL RESPONSE, available for $6.95 from SON-RISE Publications, Rte. 3, P.O. Box 202, New Wilmington, PA. 16142, Phone=412-946-8334. (Please tell them we recommended the book).

You may also contact Cathedral Of Praise to order a tape by my friend Dr. Alan Langstaff, who has also pleaded with David Hunt, concerning his cannibalism. Write: Cathedral of Praise, 10333 W. 70th Street, Eden Prarie, MN., 55344 for the tape, "Reply To Seduction of Christianity." Cost-$3.50.

WHAT DO YOU THINK?

In what way have you benefited from reading this book, *THE CULT OF CANNIBALS?* Can you see how the Biblical principles presented here can apply to a response to a book such as *Seduction*? We would like to know if you have been blessed and edified by your reading, and we invite a response from you.

Write: John Roy Bohlen, Great Commission Ministries, P.O. Box 7123, Minneapolis, MN., 55407

CHAPTER 13 - REVIEW
"SEDUCTION"

1. Do you agree that these authors of *"SEDUCTION"* should have made the effort to contact those whom they publicly criticized?

2. In your humble opinion, what is meant by the Bible phrase, "touched the Lord's anointed"?

3. Do you think that "visualization" is a valid concept?

4. Do you agree that "meditation" can be good?

5. Comment on the continuum graph we made going from "it's of the devil" on the one hand to a "thus saith the Lord" on the other.

6. Do you have a Godly fear, lest you become guilty of "touching the Lord's anointed"?

7. Do you think that you are teachable?

8. What do you think it means to "blaspheme the Holy Spirit"?

9. What will happen to those who blaspheme the Holy Spirit?

CHAPTER 14 — OUTLINE

GOD'S PRIORITIES

I. HERE'S A QUESTION

II. THE INVITATION

III. THE CHALLANGE

IV. THE PLUMBLINE

V. THE IOWA FARM BOY

VI. MESSING WITH THE WORD OF GOD

VII. FACED WITH THE FACTS!

VIII. LET YOUR FINGERS DO THE TALKING

IX. THE MOST IMPORTANT THING

X. THE JUDGEMENT SEAT OF CHRIST!

XI. HELLO!

XII. REVIEW

GODS'S PRIORITIES
GOD'S DIRECTIONS:
ROAD MAP & COMPASS
or WHEN ALL ELSE FAILS - READ
THE INSTRUCTIONS!

The Holy Bible as a Book, is the most wonderful, marvelous, tremendous, powerful, informative, beautiful, precious, valuable, inspiring, anointed, helpful, instructive, inspired, revealing, nutritious, best, encouraging, edifying, uplifting, transforming, abounding, resounding, Holy, abundant, absolute, accurate, acceptable, adorable, admirable, advanced, adventurous, actualizing...., etc. BOOK IN THE WORLD TODAY!!! (At this point, I had started going through the dictionary, trying to find all the positive words to describe the greatness of the Word Of God! Wow!!! But then my friend Joel came along and rescued me from continuing on through the dictionary!) The Bible is God's lovely Love Letter to us!!!

HERE'S A QUESTION!

Please, stop for a moment, and ask yourself this question: HOW MANY HOURS, AT AN AVERAGE

SPEED OF PULPIT READING, WOULD YOU GUESS THAT IT WOULD TAKE TO READ THE ENTIRE BIBLE THROUGH??? And this question: HAVE YOU EVER READ THE BIBLE THROUGH, WITHOUT SKIPPING ANY PARTS?? (Please pause and answer these 2 questions.)

We have discovered that less than about 1 out of 100 "born-again" (the only kind there is) Christians, have ever read the Bible through without skipping any parts! And yet, at average pulpit reading speed, the whole Bible can be read aloud in only 50 to 70 hours, or so! This can be demonstrated by checking how many 60 minute tapes are in your local Christian book store's entire Bible on cassette tape. (You can read through the entire Bible in 9 months at only 15 minutes a day, or in one week at 10 hours a day, etc.!!!)

THE INVITATION - BEGIN TODAY!

We would like to plead with you that you begin today to read your Bible through, but this time a little differently. We have found that if you put the day's date at the end of each chapter read, that it helps tremendously. Here's what normally happens. One gets inspired to read the Bible and decides usually to start at the beginning. Genesis is pretty interesting and parts of Exodus, but then comes Leviticus, Numbers and other books that can be "seemingly boring", unless you approach it right. So, we suggest that you start today, putting the day's date at the end of each chapter read, as it is easy to lose one's place or the bookmark. Most people then get discouraged, until they get inspired again, but with the same results!

We also suggest that you begin with the New Testament, unless you have read it through recently. Don't skip any parts, as it's all a part of the LOVE LETTER from God to YOU! Most people have a spastic, "hit and miss" pattern of Bible reading, and you may still do this, if you like, but NOT as a substitute for programing the spiritual computer of your heart and soul and mind and spirit and emotions, through regular, progressive and systematic reading of God's Word!!! Computer geniuses tell me that it is still impossible to get out of a computer what has not been programed into it, and though we have the Lord's lovely promise that He will "bring all things to our remembrance," yet God has not promised to bring to our remembrance Scriptures that we never "remembranced" in the first place!

THE CHALLENGE

We would like to invite you to go through your Bible with this project in mind, if you will. LET EVERY THING YOU BELIEVE, BE CHANGED TO LINE UP WITH WHAT YOU READ IN GOD'S WORD. Will you? "For I testify unto every man that heareth the Words of the Prophecy of This Book, (the Bible), If ANY one shall add unto these things, Yahweh (God) SHALL add unto him the plagues that are written in This Book:"! "And if any one shall take away from the Words of the Book of this Prophecy, Yahweh SHALL take away his part out of the Book of

Life, and out of the Holy City, and from the things which are written in this Book...Surely I come suddenly."!!! Revelation 22. So, this time as you go through the Bible, will you commit yourself to make your thinking and doctrine agree with God and His Holy WORD??!

THE PLUMBLINE

I saw a cartoon picturing an official delegation ready to cut the ribbon on a bridge opening ceremony, with the cars lined up, and the band ready to play, while off to one side the construction engineers were looking at some blueprints. The end of the bridge was 10 feet short of the mark! One builder said to the other, "I guess that WAS a fly speck after all!"

You see, we get into trouble when we depart from the Bible's formula that God gives us to help us walk with Him. If our response is, "heifer dust and fly specks" when we depart from the formula God gives us to help us walk with Him.... If our response is, "heifer dust and fly specks", when God tells us to put one foot in front of the other, then we'll miss the mark too.

"DIVISIONS AND FIGHTINGS AMONG YOU"

Paul talks of the cannibalism among us. But most of it will stop IF we can agree to very simply DO what the Bible says to DO!!!

There are two basic approaches to the Word of God when we see a high and lofty standard: 1) Most folks seem to say, "I really don't see this happening in my life, or in the lives of those around me, or this verse doesn't make sense to me, or agree with my doctrine or theology or church nor is it CONVENIENT - THEREFORE what it REALLY must mean is......." Then we explain it in terms that no longer convict or challenge us or require us to DO the will of God. This, of course, is WRONG!

The second and proper approach is one that I took as a barefoot Iowa farm boy. That approach says, "Lord Jesus, this is what Your Word says. I haven't seen this done, and I don't know how to walk in this, but I believe it because You say it. Therefore, make my life to conform with what Your Word says!!!" Then, instead of me compromising the Word down to my level, God beautifully raises my life and experience to conform to the level of His expectancy for me!!! Wow! What an adventure!

THE IOWA FARM BOY

My older sister Sherrill once had a very brainy boy friend who was a straight "A" graduate of George Washington University. He was also into a spastic brand of pseudo-intellectual theology that pretended that there were "inconsistencies" in the Bible. When he would come around, he would also bring his "inconsistencies". Each time, I would listen patiently to his "thing". And then, I would take my Bible and go to be alone in the hay loft or out under the stars, and simply ask the Lord to show me the answer to these. And each time God would show me.

For example: "How could Judas in one place go out and hang himself (Mat.27), and also 'fall

296

headlong and have his insides gush out'?" (Acts 1) So, the Lord showed me, "The rope broke!" Here's another one: "How could the genealogy of Christ in the Gospel of St Matthew be the genealogy also of Christ in St Luke, since they are so different?" Came the answer back from the Lord to this simple teenage Iowa farm boy, "One was the ancestry of Christ through Mary and one was through Joseph, the step-father, but through whom the legal line would come!" The genealogies couldn't possibly be the same!!!

But, later on, I came up against something I wasn't quite prepared for. Riding on a bus back to St Louis from a kid's camp, sponsored by a liberal church, I was quoting an innocent Scripture from Romans, when my brainy sister's boyfriend hit me with a new one. He said, "Why, that's not for today!" I said, "What?" Boyfriend said, "Yeah! An' if you don't believe me, go ask that evangelist over there." Sure enough, this "liberal evangelist" solemnly nodded his head and said in a very pious sounding tone, "Yes, that's not for today!" He said, "that's why we need the HolyGoz'; to help us figure out what's for us and what ain't, what's for today and what ain't!" I went up to the front of the bus and began thinking about this, and the more I thought about it the more filled with despair I became, because I thought "I'm going to have to spend the rest of my life trying to figure out what's for today and what is not?"

"MESSING WITH THE WORD OF GOD"

I Corinthians in the Bible is a classic example. Though all of the books are for ALL of us, yet some of the letters begin, addressed as though to someone else, although they are really and truly to us! BUT THERE IS ONE BOOK ESPECIALLY MARKED FOR US so strongly as to leave absolutely no room for question!!! It is I Corinthians! Yet, there is no other Book in the Bible more disputed, divided, cut up, cut out, forgotten or fought over than this one!

For example, in chapter 1, it says, "..To them that are sanctified in Christ Jesus, called saints, WITH ALL THAT IN EVERY PLACE call upon the Name of Jesus Christ our Lord, BOTH THEIRS AND OURS."!!!

In other words, God makes it VERY clear that this Book is for all the Christians everywhere.

FACED WITH THE FACTS!!!

I have a question. If you saw in God's Word that you were believing incorrectly, would you have the courage or integrity or dedication or willingness to change? Most do not and will not. But if we are going to walk with God, we must!

In I Corinthians 5 & 6, it talks about the Scriptural principle of quarantine, but I heard this week about a woman who was awarded over $200,000 for being excluded from a church for continuing her adultery!!!

Now, look with me at how inconsistent we have been in our reading of the Scriptures. Got your scissors handy? The first half of I Corinthians 11 talks about head covering, and the last half presents Holy Communion (and unholy, too,). Chapter 12 portrays the importance of apostles and speaking in tongues. Thirteen is the famous love chapter. Fourteen speaks of tongues, interpretation of tongues and women. And fifteen speaks of the resurrection!

LET YOUR FINGERS DO THE TALKING

Let the fingers of your left hand illustrate each of these five chapters, bending them half way or totally down as you like. Most "Christians" (to all of whom these chapters apply,) REJECT the part about the head covering, ("old fashioned, I guess) but KEEP the part about Holy and unholy communion, REJECT the importance of apostles and tongues-speaking, ("why's an apostle needed, anyway"?), INCLUDE the "Love chapter" - " 'cause ev'rbody loves love", REJECT chapter 14 " 'cause we're talkin' interpretation of tongues and women again, but" (are you bending your fingers down, or using your scissors, as you reject these?) "let's KEEP the chapter about the resurrection 'cause every body wants to live forever!" (except in hell! "Yah, while we're at it let's pour water on that, too, 'cauz hell's prob'ly hot").

Tell me, what favorite Scripture have you "reasoned away" or said "that's not for today", just because it wasn't "convenient" or taught in your church??? Can you see the illogicality and gross inconsistency of this silly selectivity. The snake in the Garden still whispers into the ears of the modern-day Eve's and Adam's, "Hath God said?"

But we recommend that you and I NOT try to "msliberal-reason" it or "fundy-dispensationalate" it away, or otherwise try to cut up or "mess" with the

Sword of the Word, or we're liable to get a bad ow-ee. Agree? What does the good book say, "Them who cut-up will get cut up"? Not "caught up" - CUT up. Pretty sharp, eh? Remember, the Word of God is a SHARP TWO EDGED Sword - that is it cuts both ways!!!

My friend Leonard Ravenhill, in his book *Why Revival Tarries,* says, "One of these days, some simple soul will pick up the Word of God, read it, and BELIEVE it, and then the rest of us will be embarrassed!" Why, just think of it. Some simple soul might read I Corinthians, (if he hasn't been taught otherwise in some "the illogical cemetary") and after reading I Corinthians might start speaking in tongues, prophesying, without a head covering, become a desperately needed apostle and even start raising people from the dead!!! (I Cor.11 to 15). What would really be a miracle is if, on top of all this, God could even get him to love people as in chapter 13!!!

THE MOST IMPORTANT THING
or
GOD'S PRIORITIES
or
HAMARTANO

I used to be into gun shooting, knife throwing, archery, churiken and sling shots, etc. As a kid on the Iowa farm, we supplemented our food supply with rabbit and squirrel meat and we used to aim for the eye so as not to waste meat. But if we missed the target by more than an inch, then we missed the target!

Guess where the expression "bull's eye" came from. But now I'm into "the weapons of our warfare" that "are MIGHTY through God!!!" Some Scriptures on this are: Sweet Psalm 149, I Cor.9:7, II Cor.10:4, & I Tim.1:18. (See also our book, *HOW TO RULE THE WORLD or SEEK 1ST THE KINGDOM OF GOD!* There were men of God who were able to hit a target and not miss "by a hair's breadth" (Judges 20:16 & I Chron.12:2.) Paul said, "Forgetting every thing else, I press towards the MARK for the PRIZE of THE HIGH CALLING of God in Christ Jesus!!!"

The most often used word for sin in the Bible is a Greek word Hamartano. (All of the a's are pronounced like, "open your mouth and say 'ah' ", emphasis on tan, and then o as in oh!) Hamartano means "to miss the mark or to miss the bull's eye!"

You know the place on the bull's eye target I hate the most? You guessed it! The part right next to the center ring! Because, if I miss the bull's eye, I've MISSED! 'Cauz this ain't horse shoes, (Mizz, MISS, or "missed her", as the case may be).

On the Judgement Day, we will be held responsible for only two things: 1) Did we hit the mark, or the bull's eye of the Will or Plan or Blueprint or Destiny of God for our life, and 2) Did we do God's will for our life with a sweet spirit or a positive attitude or a right heart.

The Bible says that we are "saved" or "born again" by simply accepting Jesus Christ within, to be our Lord and Saviour and Master by simply inviting Him within to take over completely to forgive all sin and

301

give us the free gift of His Salvation from sin, selfishness, futility and hell. He actually BECOMES our Salvation! But THE REASON we become born anew IS SO THAT WE WILL DO THE PLAN & BLUEPRINT & WILL OF GOD & HIS DESTINY FOR OUR LIVES!!! Ephesians 2:8-10 says this same thing.

In other words, God has planned for us a whole life time of LIVING WORKS and CREATIVE WORDS for us to do and speak!!! Glorious Adventure! Exhilarating Thrill! Actualized Potential! Greatest Opportunity! Unsailed Seas! Uncharted Territory! Fabulous Experiences! Exciting Plans! Futility Gone! Fulfillment Fulfilled! Unexplored Explorations!

Soon, we will all be tested on how much we did of His plan for us.

THE JUDGEMENT SEAT OF CHRIST!!!

"For we must ALL appear before the Judgement Seat of Christ, That EVERYONE will receive the things done in the body, according to what you have done, whether it be good or bad. Knowing therefore, THE TERROR OF THE LORD, we persuade men..."!!! II Cor.5.

Heb. 10:31 - "It is a fearful thing to fall into the hands of the Living God!!!"

Like the song goes, "FOREVER IS A LONG, LONG TIME TO BURN!!!!!"

Wise Solomon reduced it down for us to it's simplest form. God spoke through him, "Let us hear the conclusion of the whole matter: 'Fear God, and keep His commandments: for this is the whole duty of man. For God shall bring every work into judgement, with every secret thing, whether it be good, or whether it be evil." Ecclesiastes 12:13 & 14.

We have seen how God will bring horrible judgement upon all of us who cannibalize others in the body of Christ, for IT SHALL BE ACCREDITED TO OUR ACCOUNT, AS HAVING BEEN DONE TO CHRIST, THE WAY WE RELATE TO EVEN THE LEAST OF THOSE WHO ARE DOING THE WILL OF GOD!!!

But it can be simplified even more! "Master, which is the great (that is, the greatest) commandment in the law? Jesus said unto him, 'THOU SHALT LOVE THE LORD THY GOD WITH ALL THY HEART, AND WITH ALL THY SOUL, AND WITH ALL THY MIND. THIS IS THE FIRST AND GREAT-(EST) COMMANDMENT And the second is like unto it, THOU SHALT LOVE THY NEIGHBOR AS THYSELF!!! ON THESE TWO COMMANDMENTS HANG ALL THE LAW AND THE PROPHETS! Matthew 23:36-40.' "

HELLO, MY BROTHER! HELLO, MY SISTER!

Jesus said that it will be accredited to our account, as having been done to Christ, the way we relate to even the least of His "brethren"! And who did He say that His brethren are? He said, "My mother, brother and sister is he or she that DOES THE WILL OF MY FATHER!" And that's who our mother, brother or sister is today, also! (Matthew 25 & ch 12). Hello, my brother! Hello, my sister! I love you!!!

As I said to some fellow elders in an elders' meeting one time during a h'ated discussion, "Dear ones, please, there's no law against love. So please, let's just love each other!" You know what? They did not take my advice, and their church has been on a down hill slide ever since. It's really very simple isn't it.

Some folks would recommend that evangelism and testifying are the most important things, but the greatest witness of all is our love. For Jesus says, "By this shall all men know that ye are My disciples, if ye have LOVE ONE TO ANOTHER!!!" John 13:35.

And now we conclude with this thought. It is not enough that we only tolerate or accept or like or even love each other, but the commandment is given to us from God Himself in the Holy Bible, in I Peter 1:22 and 4:8. "Seeing that ye have purified your souls in obeying the Truth through the Spirit unto unfeigned love of the brethren, SEE THAT YE LOVE ONE ANOTHER WITH A PURE HEART FER-VENTLY!!!" (Fervently means with white hot burning intensity)! And here is the first and the final Word: "AND ABOVE ALL THINGS HAVE FERVENT LOVE AMONG YOURSELVES."

CHAPTER 14 — REVIEW

1. What did Solomon say was the whole conclusion of the matter of life, the "whole duty of man"?

2. What reason did Solomon give for this conclusion to which he came?

3. Please complete this Kingdom Principle, "It is accredited to our account, as having been done to Christ."

4. On what commandments can be "hung" all of the law and all of the prophets?

5. Jesus said that by what would "all men know that you are" His disciples?

6. I Peter says that we are to love each other. How are we to love each other?

EPILOGUE

AND THE HUMPTY DUMTPY HEARTS LIVED HAPPILY EVER AFTER

A man of God once said to us through his tears, "Listen, can you hear them crying?" He was talking one Sunday Morning about the hearts and souls across the land that were still hurting from the night before. I worked for several years as a counsellor for the CBN 700 Club. The first call I got was from a teen-age girl who had just taken apparently a whole bottle of "red devils", or Seconal, and was just calling to say "good-bye" to someone just before she died. Fortunately, we were able to trace the call and get to her in time. Another true story tells of a person who wa walking onto a bridge where they planned to end it "Humpty Dumpty" style. But as he (or she) was walking onto the bridge, they were passed by a born-again Christian who simply smiled and said, "Hello", and walked on by. That Christian's smile alone caused a realization that life was not entirely hopeless; and that Humpty Dumpty friend changed his mind, found Christ, later met the person with the smile, and they lived happily ever after!

Have you ever been lonely? It's a strange thing indeed, that sometimes the most unloveable, need love the most. Our Lord talks about a wonderful ministry we are all called to be a part of — A sweet

sweet ministry of God's love — to Help Heal Hurting Humpty Dumpty hearts!!! Have you ever been lonely? lonely even in a crowd? Has your heart of emotion ever hurt so bad you thought it would tear out your throat? You are called to the most wonderful ministry of all — the ministry of encouragement to others. Our commission from the Lord Jesus and the Loving Heart of the Heavenly FAther is that we can "comfort others with the Love with which we have been comforted." Please pray this prayer with me:

"Dear Heavenly Father, I repent for every form of cannibalism that I have ever practiced, and for every time that I tried to practice Christian witchcraft of psychic intimidation. I am determined before You God, to never again "touch Your anointed" or to blaspheme Your Holy Spirit. I know that my treatment of Your dear ones, is accredited to my account, as having been done to Christ, and I always want to rightly relate to You, dear Lord, within Your dear ones. I also declare war against cannibalization, in my presence, of Your little children. From now on, live Your life through me; love, with Your love through me; be all that You are through me, in Jesus's Name, Amen.

GOD HAS A VISION
WE HAVE A VISION
I HAVE A VISION
PLEASE, HAVE OUR VISION

God's vision is to see the Gospel of the Kingdom preached to the uttermost part of the world. The desire of our hearts for this book and for our tapes, articles and other books is to open opportunities to present the Good News of Kingdom of God principles to those who would present the Good News of the Kingdom of God to those who would present the Good News of the Kingdom of God!!! The Apostle Paul commanded, "The things that you have heard and received from me, commit thou to faithful ones, who shall be able to teach others, also."

Would you seek God? Would you seek God very earnestly? Would you seek God from your heart to see whether or not you will share this vision? Would you seek God deep in your heart to make God's vision — THE GREAT COMMISSION — YOUR VISION???

As we have stated before, our whole desire is to do God's will. If we can be of any help, in any way that will promote the Kingdom of God on earth, please call on us. Our present address is: The Great Commission Ministries, P.O. 7123, Minneapolis, MN., 55407. Any checks made out to either "The Great Commission" or "The Kingdom of God" are tax deductible, and will be used for the fulfillment of the ministry of spreading the Gospel of the Kingdom. We thank God for your response to His Divine Call to the Dynamic Destiny of Discipleship!!!

There are available to you representatives of the Kingdom of God to come to your area for classes, seminars, sermons, on more than the following areas, including the material taught in this book: Marriage and family, Discipleship training, the Lordship of Christ, the Fullness of God, Church Growth and

Renewal, Worship, and The KINGDOM OF GOD. We will try to put you in touch with them if you don't know where to find them

THE GREAT COMMISSION

The God of all Heaven and Earth speaks to you now, a crystal clear, pure and sure, thus saith the Lord, "SEEK YE FIRST THE KINGDOM OF GOD, AND HIS RIGHTEOUSNESS; AND ALL THESE THINGS WILL BE ADDED UNTO YOU!!!"

GO YE THEREFORE AND TEACH [MAKE DISCIPLES OF] ALL NATIONS, BAPTIZING THEM IN THE NAME OF THE FATHER, AND OF THE SON, AND OF THE HOLY SPIRIT; TEACHING THEM TO OBEY ALL THINGS WHATSOEVER I HAVE COMMANDED YOU. AND LO, I AM WITH YOU ALWAYS, EVEN UNTO THE END OF THE WORLD. AMEN. (Mat. 28:20).

KINGDOM QUESTIONS
(PLEASE RESPOND)

1. Do you know of anyone that could benefit from any part of the Kingdom of God in terms of counselling, prayer, training, personal ministry, visitation, encouragement, seminars or additional copies of this book, etc.?

2. Do you know of any source that has abilities or resources or money that you or they would like to volunteer for the cause of the advancement of the Gospel of the Kingdom?

3. Do you personally have any gifts or abilities time or talents, money or possessions that you would be willing to volunteer to the cause of Christ as it relates to the Kingdom of God and to the spreading of the Gospel of the Kingdom? On a short term basis; or long term; or monthly basis?

4. Do you know of any group or church that could benefit in any way from the resources of the Kingdom of God in terms of retreats, conferences, meetings, seminars, teaching, Bible studies, speakers, etc.?, on the subjects of Discipleship-Leadership Training, Church Growth and Renewal, Marriage and Family, The Kingdom of God, etc.?

5. Do you have any constructive counsel for this presentation? Other ideas for the outreach of the Gospel of the Kingdom? Anything to offer that would be of help?

6. Would you be interested in fellowship or getting

to know others that also have an unreserved discipleship commitment to Jesus Christ the Lord and King?

7. Are you willing to give and live your life completely to the King of Kings, and Lord of lords, to seek first the Kingdom of God and His righteousness?

8. Has this book been a blessing to you? We would like to know.

9. Would you be interested in contributing or helping to get this book into the hands of those not able to pay for it, i.e., the poor, "shut-in's," prisoners, other countries, students, hospitalized, etc.?

10. Do you know of anyone who would like this book on tape or in another language, or of anyone who would be willing to translate this book into another language?

11. Would you like a copy or copies of the Kingdom Contract evangelism brochure?

12. Would you like to have additional copies of this book? It was designed for use in any of the following ways: Seminary, Bible College, Bible School, Sunday School, Seminars, Conferences, Church Renewal, Discipleship-Leadership Training, Personal Study, Family Devotions, Home Meetings, Classroom Curriculum, Men's or Women's Meetings, Sermon or Teaching Series, publication in periodicals, etc.

13. Would you like to be kept informed of new books or developments relating to the ministry of the Great Commission?

OPPORTUNITY!

All correspondence may be directed to:
The Great Commission Ministries
c/o John Bohlen, a representative
P.O. Box 7123
Minneapolis, Minnesota 55407

This book is also available on tape cassettes.
(All gifts to The Great Commission Ministries are tax deductible) You may make checks out to: The Kingdom of God!

You can help fulfill the Great Commission through book sales and distribution, along with other Christian Bibles, books, tapes, and records, while at the same time obtaining your own material at a discount or for profit to you and your organization.

If you cannot afford to pay for these products, please let us know so we can look to the Lord together to see if we can work something out. O.K.???!!!

TAPE INDEX

"BOHLEN FAMILY SINGERS": JOEY, KARI DAWN JOY, JOSHUA, JOHN & KAREN — This is a tape of various "Gaither Style" songs made several years ago, of the Bohlen Family singing. John & Karen also "Do a duet", Joshua sings, etc.

"EVERYONE HAS A PSALM: I COR. 14:26 EQUIP THE SAINTS" — So many in the Body of Christ are "Drowning in their own pew", and have not been equipped. This tape presents the vision that every member in the body of Christ is called to be a minister, and shows how to get started.

FEAST OF TABERNACLES: INTRODUCTION
— by John Roy Bohlen

"HELPING HEAL HURTING HUMPTY DUMPTY HEARTS" —So many of the dear ones are hurting. But the King's men haven't been putting these hurting ones back together again. Here's how we can!

"HOW TO GET & KEEP A RIGHT SPIRIT"

HOW TO RAISE 'PURFECT' KIDS! The book on tape!

"HOW TO RULE THE WORLD! THE BOOK": 4 tapes. This is the book on tape, word for word, without comments. Tapes #5 to 8.

CULT OF CANNIBALS This is another book on tape, simply read, without comment. The title is a take off on Paul's warning: "Be careful, dear ones, lest you bite and devour one another, and are consumed by each other."

JOHN SINGS: Tape #1 (this is not a "professional" recording,—just simply, from the heart.)

JOH, JOSH, ETC. SINGS: A song book on tape (4 tapes-nearly 300 songs)

"THE KING'S GREATEST SECRET!" Want to be perfect? Here's how!

MESSIANIC VISION: RAIDO BROADCAST: Sid Roth — Interviews on the book, *"Rule the World."* Sid is alive!

DISCIPLESHIP SEMINAR: Video sound track — This seminar on discipleship uses the book *How To Rule The World.* 2 hours.

YOUR SEXUAL MINISTRY, This is a book on marriage. We simply read it on tape.

LITERATURE

HOW TO RULE THE WORLD, John's 1st book, this one is a handbook on The Kingdom Of God.

WORKBOOK STUDY MANUAL FOR THE BOOK, HOW TO RULE THE WORLD

YOUR SEXUAL MINISTRY, For marrieds only, or those about to be, this marriage manual deals with far more than the sexual aspects of marriage. Here's how you who are married can live happily ever after!!!

HOW TO RAISE 'PURFECT' KIDS, Kingdom keys for raising Kingdom kids.

If you are on our mailing list, we will keep you informed as other tapes, sermon outlines, song books, articles, etc., become available.

These materials are available to you, as Yahweh provides. Are you willing to ask heavenly Father if He will allow you, as a Great Commission Ministry, to regularly contribute toward spreading the gospel of the Kingdom!!! THANK YOU!

GOD'S SWEET BEST TO YOU — ALWAYS!